主 编◎吴勇毅 副主编◎刘 弘

School: _____

Grade/Class: _____

Name: _____

China Study 9

中国研习

王佳艺 刘艳辉◎译

Nicholas Thomas Zazzi ◎审

华东师范大学出版社

·上海·

图书在版编目（CIP）数据

中国研习.九年级＝China Study. Grade Nine:
汉英对照 / 吴勇毅主编；王佳艺，刘艳辉译. — 上海:
华东师范大学出版社，2019
ISBN 978-7-5675-9870-6

Ⅰ.①中…　Ⅱ.①吴…　②王…　③刘…　Ⅲ.①汉语—
对外汉语教学—教材　Ⅳ.①H195.4

中国版本图书馆CIP数据核字（2019）第263995号

中国研习（九年级）
China Study (Grade Nine)

主　　编　吴勇毅
副主编　刘　弘
策划编辑　王　焰
项目编辑　龚海燕　种道旸
责任编辑　顾晨溪
责任校对　曹　勇　时东明
装帧设计　卢晓红

出版发行　华东师范大学出版社
社　　址　上海市中山北路3663号　邮编 200062
网　　址　www.ecnupress.com.cn
电　　话　021-60821666　　行政传真 021-62572105
客服电话　021-62865537　　门市（邮购）电话 021-62869887
地　　址　上海市中山北路3663号华东师范大学校内先锋路口
网　　店　http://hdsdcbs.tmall.com/

印 刷 者　上海邦达彩色包装印务有限公司
开　　本　889×1194　16开
印　　张　13.25
字　　数　143千字
版　　次　2021年9月第1版
印　　次　2021年9月第1次
书　　号　ISBN 978-7-5675-9870-6
定　　价　88.00元

出 版 人　王　焰

　　《中国研习》是一套为国际学校 1-12 年级外籍学生开发的中国文化与社会探究教材。本套教材的编写参考了国际文凭课程（IB课程）大纲，并且吸收了教育部基础教育课程教材发展中心（NCCT）"外籍人员子女学校认证标准"中有关中国文化课程教学的要求。教材采取探究式教学方法，并为该课程研发了数字教育平台，力求创造轻松愉快的学习环境，培养学生开放的、包容的批判性思维能力。

　　全套教材共分成小学、初中和高中三个系列。小学系列共有 6 册，初中和高中系列各有 3 册。每册有 12 个单元，每个单元涉及一个主题，教师可以根据学校的课时安排每周或者若干周学习一个单元，也可以根据教学需要挑选其中某个单元来使用。

　　本套教材具有如下几个主要特点：

1. 以主题方式编写教材

　　主题式教学是以内容为载体、以文本的内涵为主题所进行的一种教学活动。本套教材的主题尽量考虑到国际学校学生在学习、生活中可能会遇到的各种社会文化内容，并且有意识养成学生能对母国文化和中国文化进行比较和思考的习惯，以培养学生的国际情怀。

2. 以探究式活动来组织教材内容编排，便于师生使用

　　中国研习作为一门跨学科探究性课程，兼顾学科内的知识和跨学科领域的知识。为此，本套教材在呈现方式上以探究、活动等多维度方式为主，而非传统的简单的内容灌输施教形式；强调在各种探究活动中帮助学生内化吸收相关的知识和能力，包括不同学科的知识；鼓励学生成为学习的主体，教师则在学

生的学习中起到有效的引导作用。

3. 教材所涉及的中国文化和社会的领域十分广泛

为适应国际学校有关中国社会及文化课程的需要，本套教材所涉及的内容不仅仅局限于狭义的中国文化范畴，而是扩展到中国艺术（包括音乐、戏剧、视觉艺术等），政治，经济，历史，地理，科学（包括数学、物理、化学等）等多方面，这与IB课程要跨学科、内容要涉及多种学科领域的理念是一致的。我们认为，中国文化教学不仅是中文教师的工作，其他学科的教师也完全可以参与其中，也唯有如此，才能真正使得文化通识在国际教育环境下扎根。这种跨学科的教学，也符合IB等国际教育中强调的"课程融合"理念。

4. 提供具体的评价指标，便于教师对于学生的表现作出评价

为了适应活动探究的教学需要，本套教材鼓励教师以过程化的档案袋评价方式为主。教师通过对学生在不同阶段的学习过程和学习结果进行评估，及时对学生的学习表现作出反馈并提出改进意见，从而在教学过程中更好地激发学生的兴趣，调动学生的学习主动性，引导他们学习、理解、研究和探索，让学生成为主导自己的主人。

5. 中英文对照编辑，适应多种需要

考虑到国际学校学生汉语水平和课程教学的多样性特点，本套教材采取中英文对照形式，这样既可以满足国际学校基于内容的汉语教学的需要，也可以供国际学校教授其他课程的教师参考或补充教学，还可以作为师生的课外活动手册。此外，教材中将重要文化知识和内容要点列出，也便于学生自学使用。

本套教材的研发团队来自华东师范大学等知名高校和多所国际学校，不仅

包括拥有丰富教学经验和较高理论水平的高校专业教师，还吸收了一部分国际学校一线的教学和管理人员。其核心成员参加过国际汉语教学相关标准、大纲和教材的研发工作，对于各类国际学校常用标准、大纲和课程有过专门研究，在国内外发表过相关的研究成果，具有丰富的课程设计和教材编写经验。

希望通过学习和使用本套教材，能够使更多的国际学生认识中国、了解中国。

吴勇毅

2021 年 9 月

China Study is a set of Chinese culture and social inquiry textbooks designed for foreign students of international schools in grades 1–12. Based on the IB syllabus, this set of textbooks has absorbed the teaching requirements of "certification standards of school for foreign children" developed by National Center for School Curriculum and Textbook Development (NCCT), Ministry of Education. The textbooks adopt an exploration-based teaching method and provide a digital education platform, attempting to create a relaxing and enjoyable learning environment and to develop students' critical thinking skills.

This set of textbooks is divided into three series: elementary school, junior high school and senior high school. There are 6 volumes in the elementary school series and 3 volumes in the junior high school and senior high school series respectively. There are 12 units in each volume and every unit deals with a specific theme. Teachers can teach one unit for each week or several weeks according to class schedule, or select one of the units to use according to requirements.

This set of textbooks has the following main features:

1. Theme-related teaching method

Theme-related teaching method is based on the content and the connotation of each unit. This set of textbooks takes into account the various social and cultural contents that international school students may encounter in their study and life, and intends to cultivate students' habit of comparing and thinking about their native culture and Chinese culture in order to cultivate their international mindedness.

2. Exploratory activities to facilitate teachers' and students' use

China Study is an interdisciplinary exploration course that intends to incorporate knowledge within the discipline and knowledge in interdisciplinary fields. To this end, this set of textbooks is based on exploration, activities and other multi-dimensional ways rather than simply cramming knowledge into students' heads. We emphasize on students' ability to absorb knowledge of different subjects through various exploration activities. We also encourage students to become the initiator of learning and teachers to play an effective guiding role in students' learning.

3. Covering a wide range of Chinese culture and society

In order to meet the needs of the international school curriculum on Chinese society and culture, the content of this set of textbooks is not limited to the narrow Chinese culture category but extended to Chinese art (including music, opera, visual arts, etc.), politics, economy, history, geography, science (including mathematics, physics, chemistry, etc.) and many other aspects—consistent with the concept that IB courses should be interdisciplinary and involve multiple subjects. We believe that Chinese culture teaching is not only the work for Chinese teachers, and teachers from other disciplines can also participate in Chinese culture teaching. Only in this way can cultural education take root in an international education environment. This interdisciplinary teaching is also in line with the "curricular integration" concept emphasized in international education such as IB.

4. Providing specific evaluation means for students' performance

In order to meet the needs of activity exploration, this set of textbooks encourages teachers to focus on process evaluation. Teachers evaluate students' learning process and results at different stages, and give timely feedback and suggestions to students' learning performance so as to evoke students' interest in study and guide them to further understand, research and explore Chinese culture.

5. Editing in both Chinese and English to meet various needs

Taking into consideration the diversity of Chinese language proficiency and curriculum teaching in international schools, this set of textbooks offers both Chinese and corresponding English translations. This can meet the needs of content-based Chinese language teaching in international schools, as well as the needs of international school teachers who teach other courses. It can also be used as a manual for extracurricular activities. In addition, important cultural knowledge and content points are listed in the textbook, which is also convenient for students to study by themselves.

The writers of this set of textbooks come from well-known universities such as East China Normal University (ECNU) and many international schools. They include professional teachers with rich teaching experience and high theoretical level, and also some front-line teaching and management personnel from international schools. Among them, the core members have participated in the development of relevant standards, syllabus and textbooks for international Chinese teaching and have conducted special research on these fields with relevant results published at home and abroad.

We hope that by studying and using this set of materials, more international students can get to know China and understand China better.

September 2021

目录

第一课
Lesson One
中国公司 / 12
Chinese Corporations / 13

第二课
Lesson Two
情景喜剧 / 26
Situation Comedy / 27

第三课
Lesson Three
中国古代数学 / 40
Mathematics in Ancient China / 41

第四课
Lesson Four
地铁 / 56
Metro System / 57

第五课
Lesson Five
中国家具 / 72
Chinese Furniture / 73

第六课
Lesson Six
中国风音乐 / 92
Chinese-Style Music / 93

Contents

第七课 / **Lesson Seven**　禁忌文化 / 108　Taboo Culture / 109

第八课 / **Lesson Eight**　网络文学 / 124　Network Literature / 125

第九课 / **Lesson Nine**　中国功夫 / 140　Chinese Kung Fu / 141

第十课 / **Lesson Ten**　中国教育 / 160　Education in China / 161

第十一课 / **Lesson Eleven**　太空科技 / 178　Space Science & Technology / 179

第十二课 / **Lesson Twelve**　中国人的婚姻 / 192　Chinese Marriages / 193

第一课　中国公司

1. 学习目标

（1）能说出一些著名的中国公司的名称。

（2）能说出一些中国公司的代表性产品。

（3）能分析一些中国公司成功的原因。

2. 热身活动

讨论

（1）你知道哪些中国公司的名字？它们主要生产哪方面的产品？

（2）你知道世界上有哪些手机公司？有没有中国的品牌？

（3）你或者你身边的人使用华为或者小米的手机吗？对这些手机评价如何？

（4）你知道中国人常说的BAT指的是哪三家公司吗？它们分别有哪些产品？

（5）你和你的朋友怎么看待中国公司的产品？

Lesson One　Chinese Corporations

1. Learning objectives

(1) Be able to name some well-known Chinese corporations.

(2) Be able to list some representative products made by Chinese corporations.

(3) Be able to analyze the reasons for the success of some Chinese corporations.

2. Warm-up

Discussion

(1) What Chinese corporations do you know? What products do they make?

(2) What do you know about international mobile phone companies? Is there a Chinese one?

(3) Do you or the people around you use HUAWEI or MI phones? What are your/their comments on them?

(4) Which three companies does BAT refer to? What are their products?

(5) What comments do you and your friends have on the products of Chinese companies?

中国手机的发展

20世纪90年代，中国还没有创立自己的手机品牌，诺基亚、摩托罗拉、爱立信三家外国企业占据了中国80%的手机市场。

2005年，中国政府批准了5家公司的手机生产项目，意味着放松了手机制造的政策。不少公司看准了这个时机，纷纷开设手机制造工厂，但由于缺少经验和技术，很多公司采用了模仿国外技术的方法来生产手机，后来被人们称为"山寨手机"。2009年随着苹果手机进入中国市场，很多山寨手机工厂纷纷倒闭。

2011年小米手机出现了。由于小米自主设计的手机符合中国人的需求，价廉物美，使得整个中国市场开始活跃起来，其他的厂商如华为、OPPO、vivo也跟着发展起来。2017年上半年，中国的国产手机在国内市场的占比达到了90.5%。同时，在国际市场上，中国品牌手机的总市场份额已经连续五年保持全球第一。

近几年，中国的国产手机在创新上下了很多功夫，很多新技术都是国产手机率先采用的，比如平行双摄像头，全面屏，手机的快充功能、双卡双待功能等。此外，在国内知名度不高的传音手机，在非洲受到了火热追捧。在非洲的

3. Reading texts

The Development of Mobile Phones in China

Back in the 1990s, China did not have its own mobile phone brands. Three foreign corporations, namely Nokia, Motorola, and Ericsson, occupied 80% of the Chinese mobile phone market.

In 2005, the Chinese government approved manufacturing of mobile phones by five Chinese companies, which signified that the government began to ease its policies on manufacturing mobile phones. Quite a few enterprises tried to seize this opportunity and build mobile phone factories. However, due to lack of experience and technology, many of them just copied the technologies from foreign enterprises resulting in so-called "copycat mobile phones". In 2009, as iPhone marched into Chinese market, these factories making copycat mobile phones closed down one by one.

In 2011, the MI phone was born. The birth of it brought vigor and vitality to the Chinese domestic mobile phone market, as the design satisfies the need of Chinese people and the quality is good enough for a low-priced phone. Following MI, other manufacturers such as HUAWEI, OPPO and vivo grew very fast. In the first half year of 2017, China's self-made mobile phones accounted for 90.5% of the domestic market. In addition, the total market share of China's self-made mobile phones ranked the first in global market for five consecutive years.

In recent years, Chinese domestic manufacturers of mobile phones have made great efforts on innovations such as the parallel dual lens camera, full screen, quick charge and double SIM functions. TECNO Mobile, a not well-known brand in China, owns over 40% market share in six major African countries.

六个主要国家中，传音手机的市场占比超过40%。中国手机逐渐得到了国人及世界的认可。

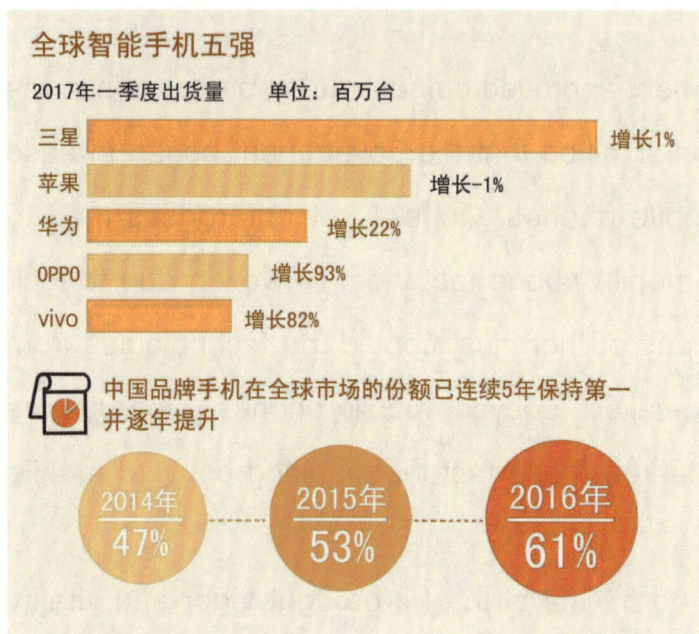

中国三大互联网巨头——BAT

BAT是中国最大的三家互联网公司，分别代表百度（Baidu）、阿里巴巴（Alibaba）和腾讯（Tencent）。

百度是全球最大的中文搜索引擎，也是最大的中文网站，于2000年1月1日创立。英国《金融时报》把百度列为"中国十大世界级品牌"，百度是这个榜单中唯一一家互联网公司，同时也是最年轻的公司。"百度"二字取自南宋词人辛弃疾的一句词：众里寻他千百度。这句话也体现了百度人对理想的执着与追

Chinese mobile phones have been gradually recognized and approved both at home and abroad.

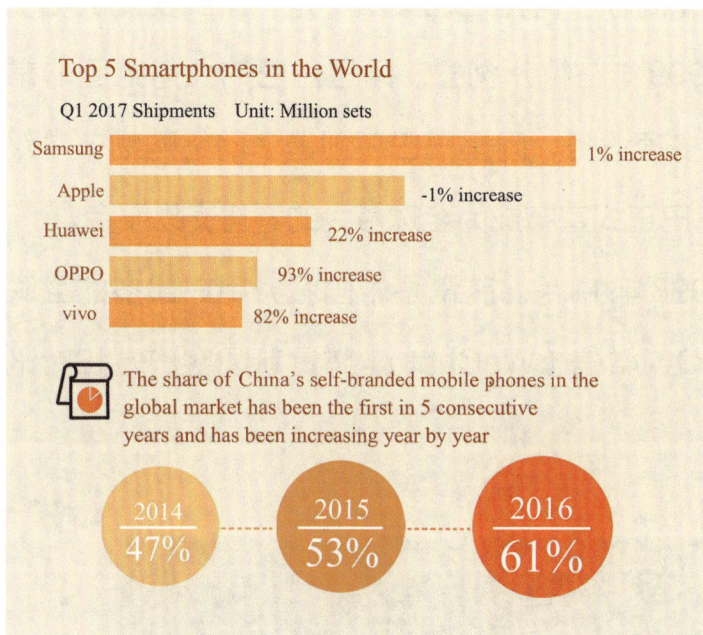

Top 5 Smartphones in the World

Q1 2017 Shipments   Unit: Million sets

Samsung	1% increase
Apple	-1% increase
Huawei	22% increase
OPPO	93% increase
vivo	82% increase

The share of China's self-branded mobile phones in the global market has been the first in 5 consecutive years and has been increasing year by year

2014 47% — 2015 53% — 2016 61%

Three Internet Giants in China—BAT

BAT refers to the three biggest Internet corporations in China, namely, Baidu, Alibaba, and Tencent.

Baidu is the biggest Chinese search engine in the world and the biggest Chinese website. It was founded on January 1, 2000. It is listed as one of the top-ten Chinese international brands by *Financial Times* and is both the only Internet company on the list and the youngest enterprise. The Chinese phrase "Baidu" is taken from the line "Zhongli xunta qianbaidu" by Xin Qiji, a poet in the Southern Song Dynasty, literally meaning looking for one among the masses for hundreds

求。百度这支中国乃至全球最优秀的技术团队，使得中国成为全球仅有的4个拥有搜索引擎核心技术的国家之一。

阿里巴巴网络技术有限公司（简称：阿里巴巴集团）是一家主要提供电子商务在线交易平台的公司，于1999年在杭州创立。阿里巴巴的业务范围非常广，包括淘宝、天猫、聚划算等多项业务，阿里巴巴还创造了网络购物节"双十一"。2016年4月6日，阿里巴巴正式宣布成为全球最大的零售交易平台。

腾讯控股有限公司成立于1998年11月。腾讯是中国服务用户最多的互联网企业之一。腾讯的服务包括QQ、微信（WeChat）、腾讯新闻客户端和腾讯视频等。

of thousands of times, which expresses the determination and persistence of Baidu staff in pursuing their dreams. Thanks to the technicians of Baidu, China has become one of the only four countries which boast the core technology for search engine.

Alibaba is a corporation providing online trading platforms for e-businesses and was founded in Hangzhou in 1999. Alibaba runs a wide range of businesses including Taobao, Tmall, Juhuasuan, etc. To attract more customers, Alibaba turns the day of "Double 11" (November 11) into an annual shopping event. Not surprisingly, on April 6, 2016, Alibaba officially announced that it became the world's biggest retail trading platform.

Tencent was founded in November 1998, and has grown into one of the Chinese Internet corporations with the largest number of customers. Its services include QQ, WeChat, Tencent news, Tencent videos, etc.

大疆无人机

　　大疆无人机是深圳大疆创新科技有限公司研发的。大疆创新科技有限公司是一家全球领先的无人飞行器控制系统及无人机解决方案的研发和生产商。

　　在许多美剧和热门电视节目中，我们都发现了大疆无人机的身影——《摩登家庭》《生活大爆炸》《神盾局特工》《苍穹之下》《全美超模大赛》……依靠着自身的创新与制造能力，大疆无人机在全球无人机中占据了大半的市场份额，全球40多个国家和地区都成为其客户。作为全球顶尖的无人机飞行平台和影像系统自主研发制造商，大疆始终以领先的技术和尖端的产品为发展核心，不仅填补了国内外多项技术空白，同时也成为同行业的领军者。

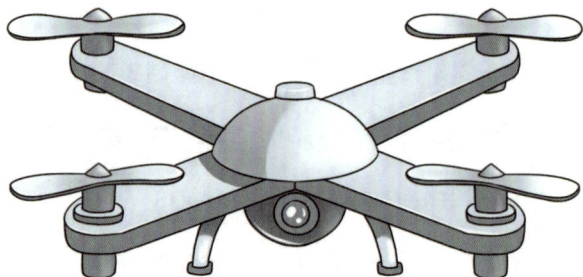

4. 重点词汇

创新

中国制造的手机有哪些**创新**之处？

搜索引擎

除了百度，你还知道哪些**搜索引擎**？

DJI Unmanned Aerial Vehicles

DJI unmanned aerial vehicles (UAVs) were developed and manufactured by SZ DJI Technology Co. Ltd, which has taken the lead in developing and providing UAV control system and solutions.

DJI UAVs made appearances in quite a lot of American dramas and TV shows such as *Modern Family*, *The Big Bang Theory*, *Agents of Shield*, *Under Dome*, and *America's Next Top Model*. Due to their innovations and manufacturing capability, DJI UAVs almost account for half of global market share with customers from over 40 countries and regions in the world. As a top manufacturer who researches and develops the flight platform and camera system of UAVs independently, DJI has been devoting to exploring innovative technologies and products, which is the core of its development strategies. Now it has become the leader in its field by filling in a gap in a few technologies both at home and abroad.

4. Keywords

innovation

What are the **innovations** of China's self-made mobile phones?

search engine

What other **search engines** do you know besides Baidu?

山寨手机

山寨手机为什么会在中国出现？又为什么会很快消失？

无人机

如果你有一架**无人机**，你想用来做什么？

5. 实践活动

（1）从下图中，你可以得到哪些信息？

国 内 厂 商 主 导 中 国 智 能 手 机 市 场
主要智能手机生产商在中国所占的市场份额（单位：出货量百分比）

■ Q2 2016　■ Q2 2017

厂商	Q2 2016	Q2 2017
华为	16.9	20.2
OPPO	16.0	18.8
vivo	13.2	17.0
小米	11.2	13.0
苹果	8.5	8.2
三星	7.0	3.0

copycat mobile phone

Why did **copycat mobile phones** appear in the Chinese market? Why did they disappear overnight?

Unmanned Aerial Vehicle (UAV)

What would you do with an **UAV** if you had one?

5. Activities

(1) Look at the following graph. What information can you get?

DOMESTIC PLAYERS DOMINATE CHINA'S SMARTPHONE MARKET

Market share of leading smartphone manufacturers in China (Unit: Precentage of shipments)

■ Q2 2016   ■ Q2 2017

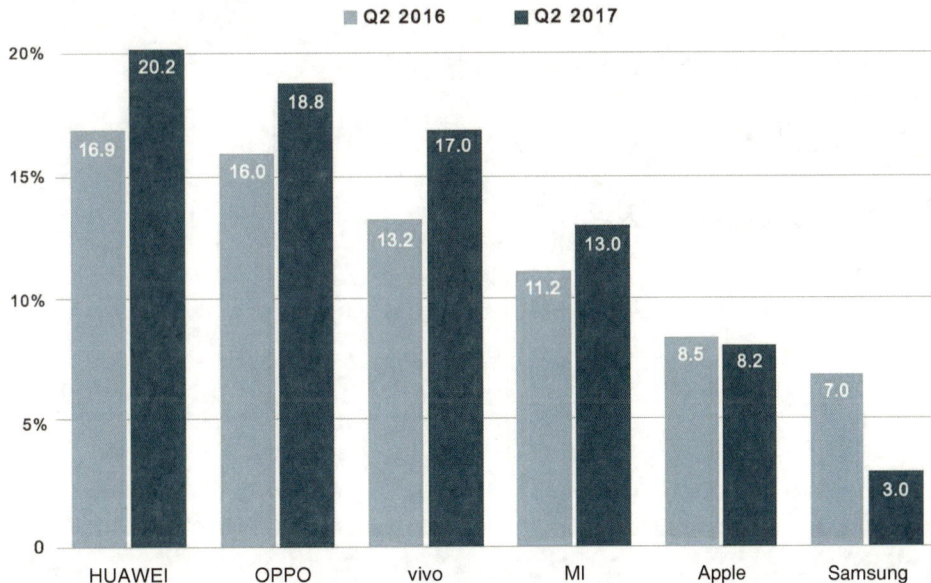

（2）中国手机的发展起步较晚，但目前市场占比最大。请查阅资料，与同学们分析为什么中国手机发展这么快。

（3）中国手机（比如华为、小米等）与苹果手机的区别是什么？你更喜欢哪个牌子的手机？为什么？

（4）BAT这三家互联网公司逐渐改变着中国人的生活方式，请试着结合这三家公司的业务，讨论BAT对中国人生活的哪些方面产生了影响。

（5）在你们国家，影响力比较大的公司有哪些？它们在哪些方面影响了人们的生活？

6. 自我评估

	😀	😐	☹️
（1）我能说出一些著名的中国公司的名称和经营领域。			
（2）我能说出中国某些产品的优点和不足。			
（3）我能分析中国公司成功的原因。			

(2) China has achieved the biggest share in the market, though it began late developing and manufacturing mobile phones. Do some research and discuss with your classmates why the mobile phone industry in China has been growing at such a rapid pace.

(3) What are the differences between iPhones and China's self-made mobile phones such as HUAWEI and MI? Which brand do you prefer and why?

(4) The three Internet corporations known as BAT have gradually changed the lifestyle of Chinese people. Discuss how BAT's businesses have been affecting Chinese people's life.

(5) What are the influential corporations in your country? How do they affect people's life?

6. Self-assessment

	☺	😐	☹
(1) I can name some well-known corporations in China and their business fields.			
(2) I can list the strengths and weaknesses of some Chinese products.			
(3) I can talk about the key to the success of some Chinese corporations.			

第二课　情景喜剧

1. 学习目标

（1）能说明情景喜剧的特点。

（2）能说明中国情景喜剧的产生和发展情况。

（3）能说明一两部中国情景喜剧的主要内容。

（4）能说明中外情景喜剧的异同。

2. 热身活动

讨论

（1）什么是情景喜剧？与其他艺术形式相比，情景喜剧有哪些特点？

（2）情景喜剧起源于哪里？你知道或者看过哪些情景喜剧？

（3）《家有儿女》是一部围绕着父母和孩子展开的情景喜剧，你们国家有类似的情景喜剧吗？请介绍一下。

（4）你认为中国人为什么能接受情景喜剧？情景喜剧要在中国成功，需要哪些条件？

Lesson Two   Situation Comedy

1. Learning objectives

(1) Be able to talk about features of situation comedy.

(2) Be able to introduce how Chinese situation comedy was born and how it developed.

(3) Be able to tell the main plot of one or two Chinese situation comedies.

(4) Be able to talk about the similarities and differences between Chinese and foreign situation comedies.

2. Warm-up

Discussion

(1) What is situation comedy? What special features does situation comedy have compared to other artistic forms?

(2) Where did situation comedy originate? Can you name or have you watched any situation comedies?

(3) Does your country have situation comedies like *Home with Kids*, which shares stories between parents and children? Please introduce one.

(4) Why do you think situation comedy is accepted by Chinese people? What are the conditions for situation comedies to succeed in China?

3. 阅读课文

情景喜剧简介

情景喜剧，是一种喜剧演出形式，起源于美国。1947年，美国播放的《玛丽·凯和琼尼》成为世界上第一部电视情景喜剧。

情景喜剧一般有固定的演员，以一条或多条故事线为中心，围绕一个或几个固定的场景进行，比如家庭、公司等。如今，情景喜剧在很多国家都很受欢迎，如《老友记》《生活大爆炸》《憨豆先生》等。

中国情景喜剧的产生与发展

（1）准备阶段

改革开放以来，中国社会发生了翻天覆地的变化。20世纪80年代中期，电视机开始进入城市家庭并逐渐普及，电视剧也在中国人的生活中变得越来越重要。1990年，长篇电视连续剧《渴望》播出，赢得了观众的好评。它不是喜剧，但是从布景、人物设置和对话中已经有情景剧的影子。1991年拍摄的《编辑部的故事》是我国第一部电视系列喜剧，更为我国情景喜剧的诞生和发展奠定了基础。

3. Reading texts

Introduction to Situation Comedy

As a genre of comedy, the situation comedy (or sitcom) was born in the USA. In 1947, the first TV sitcom, *Mary Kay and Johnny*, was broadcast in the USA.

Situation comedies usually have a continual cast of characters involved in one or a succession of stories that take place in a fixed environment, such as an apartment building or a workplace. Nowadays, situation comedies are very popular in many countries, such as *Friends*, *The Big Bang Theory* and *Mr. Bean*.

The Birth and Development of Situation Comedy in China

(1) The Preparation Stage

Since the reform and opening-up, Chinese society has undergone tremendous changes. In the middle of the 1980s, TV began to enter Chinese urban families and gradually became a common household appliance. Accordingly, watching TV dramas became a new form of entertainment and an important part of Chinese people's life. In 1990, the serial TV show *Expectation* was well received by the viewers after it was broadcast. Though *Expectation* itself is not a comedy, there are elements of a sitcom in its setting, characters, and dialogues. Shot in 1991, *Stories from the Editorial Office* was considered as China's first serial comedy on TV, which laid the foundation for the birth and development of situation comedy in China.

（2）诞生阶段

中国第一部情景喜剧《我爱我家》产生于1993年，讲述了20世纪90年代北京的一个六口之家三代人之间的生活与矛盾，不仅反映了不同人物的性格，而且透过这个小家庭发生的大事小事，展现出当时那个年代北京的生活情况。该剧的导演有意识地借鉴了情景喜剧的形式，使其成为将国外情景喜剧和中国国情相结合的一部作品。尽管当时的中国观众对于情景喜剧的"罐头笑声"和"现场录音"不太习惯，但由于剧中加入了中国观众普遍喜爱的小品形式，其一出现就大受欢迎。

（3）探索阶段

随着《我爱我家》的走红，该剧的导演于1995年开始专注于情景喜剧制作。然而1996年播出的《心理诊所》并没有取得理想的效果。1997年又推出了《中国餐馆》，讲述了美国洛杉矶的一家中国餐馆中一群留美中国人的故事，但影响力也不大。不过，此时其他电视台制作的情景喜剧却很受欢迎，比如1998年

(2) The Birth Stage

China's first situation comedy, *I Love My Home*, was first aired in 1993. It revolves around a family of six in Beijing in the 1990s. The life and conflicts of the family of three generations reflect the personalities of different characters. Moreover, what's happening in the small family, big or trivial, presents a vivid picture of how people in Beijing lived during that period of time. The director of the situation comedy borrowed features from Western sitcoms and transplanted them into the Chinese society in *I Love My Home*. Though they were not familiar with live recording and laugh tracks that were pre-recorded by a live studio audience, Chinese viewers were crazy for *I Love My Home* as soon as it was released. The elements of the Chinese sketch in the show might explain its success, since sketches were popular and loved by Chinese viewers.

(3) The Exploration Stage

After *I Love My Home* became an overnight sensation, its director began to devote himself to making sitcoms in 1995. But *The Psychological Clinic* did not seem to meet his expectations when it was broadcast in 1996; neither did *Chinese Restaurant*, a show produced in 1997 about a group of Chinese working in a Chinese restaurant in Los Angeles. On the other hand, some sitcoms shot by other TV stations turned out to be popular during the same period of time. For example, both *Old Uncle and His Sons and Grandsons* by Shanghai Dragon TV in

上海东方卫视制作播出的《老娘舅》和2000年珠江电视台制作播放的《外来媳妇本地郎》都取得了非常好的收视率。《外来媳妇本地郎》还成为唯一一个超过一千集的电视剧。后来的《东北一家人》也取得很大的成功。值得注意的是，这几部情景喜剧的成功都离不开方言和地方特色。

（4）发展阶段

2000年以来，中国的情景喜剧进入了发展期。大众对电视节目的需求持续增长，老少皆宜的情景喜剧受到观众的认可和喜爱，并且陆续出现了一些具有影响力的作品，比如《炊事班的故事》《武林外传》等。自此，中国的情景喜剧成为一种重要的电视节目形式。

《家有儿女》

《家有儿女》是一部关于少儿题材的情景轻喜剧，讲述了两个离异家庭结合后发生在父母和三个孩子间的各种趣事。该剧以浓厚的喜剧色彩、幽默的人物语言和让人忍俊不禁的剧情获得了广大电视观众的喜爱，也获得了很多奖项。

该剧其中一集讲述了一家人为夏东海准备父亲节礼物的故事。妻子刘梅想给东海惊喜，所以把事先准备

1998 and *In-Laws, Out-Laws* by Peal River TV Station in 2000 hit high audience ratings, with *In-Laws, Out-Laws* being the only Chinese sitcom with over one thousand episodes. *A Family in the Northeast* also turned out to be a big hit. It is notable that these sitcoms share one thing in common: their success is attributed to the dialects used and the local cultures they present.

(4) The Development Stage

Since 2000, sitcoms in China have been developing. With an increasing demand for TV programs by the public, sitcoms suitable for all age groups were loved by the viewers, and some of them were quite influential, such as *Story of Cooking Squad* and *My Own Swordsman*. Sitcoms have since then grown into an important kind of TV show in China.

Home with Kids

Home with Kids is a teen sitcom about three kids and their parents in a reorganized family. This sitcom has won the favor of audience for its rich colors of comedic characters, humorous language, and funny plot. Hence it has won a couple of awards.

In one of the episodes, the whole family is preparing gifts for Father's Day for Xia Donghai. To give him a surprise, Liu Mei, the wife, hides the shaver she has already bought under the sofa. Xia Xue has bought a plaster statue of

好的剃须刀藏在了沙发下；夏雪准备了维纳斯石膏像；夏雨打算送自己做的纸帽子；刘星打算送自己做的烤红薯，可是由于他闯了祸，老师要在父亲节那天家访，因此刘星用他在沙发下发现的剃须刀收买果果（刘星的同学），让果果把老师请到她家去，然而果果把剃须刀送给了夏雨。父亲节那天，刘梅拿出的礼物是刘星放的红薯，夏雨的礼物反而成了剃须刀。

《爱情公寓》

近年来，情景喜剧《爱情公寓》也深受年轻人的喜爱和欢迎。然而，此剧却引起了很大的争议。一部分人对此持支持的态度，认为此剧不仅时尚，而且每一集都有独立、完整的情节，因此从其中任何一集开始观看都是一个完整的故事。另一部分人对此持反对的态度，认为此剧主要是讲都市夜生活、纠结的感情和职场遭遇，没有价值。

4. 重点词汇

情景喜剧

世界上第一部**情景喜剧**是在哪个国家诞生的？

Venus, Xia Yu has made a paper hat by himself, while Liu Xing will cook him roasted sweet potatoes. Unfortunately, Liu Xing gets into trouble. His teacher will pay a visit to his home on Father's Day. So Liu Xing bribes Guoguo, one of his classmates, with the shaver he happens to find under the sofa to take the teacher to her home. Guoguo gives the shaver to Xia Yu. Therefore, on Father's Day when Liu Mei takes out the gift she prepares what she gets is the sweet potatoes Liu Xing hides, while the gift Xia Yu prepares turns out to be a shaver.

iPartment

In recent years, another sitcom, *iPartment* has been popular and much loved by young people. At the same time, it has aroused a heated argument among the public. Those who hold a positive attitude towards this sitcom think that this show is fashionable and each episode has its own complete plot. The audience could enjoy watching a complete story no matter which episode they choose. Those who hold a negative attitude towards this sitcom think that this sitcom has no value at all, since it only tells stories about night life in the city, agonizing feelings, and experiences at work.

4. Keywords

situation comedy/sitcom

In which country was the world's first **situation comedy/sitcom** born?

奠定

哪部作品**奠定**了中国情景喜剧的发展基础？

方言

你们国家有没有**方言**？

情节　忍俊不禁

在你看过的情景喜剧中，有哪些让你**忍俊不禁**的**情节**？

争议

《爱情公寓》引发了怎样的**争议**？观众是如何评价的？

5. 实践活动

（1）除了课文中所提到的情景喜剧，你还知道哪些？向大家介绍你最喜欢的一部情景喜剧。

（2）观看《家有儿女》的相关视频，向同学讲述你观看的那一集的故事。

（3）查找相关资料，和同学讨论一下，为什么《老娘舅》和《外来媳妇本地郎》令人耳目一新？它们有什么特点？

lay the foundation for

Which piece of work **laid the foundation for** the development of the sitcom in China?

dialect

Are there **dialects** in your country?

plot   can't help laughing

What **plots** in the sitcoms you've watched have made you **can't stop laughing**?

argument

What **argument** has *iPartment* aroused? What are the audience's comments on this sitcom?

5. Activities

(1) What other sitcoms do you know besides the ones mentioned in the texts? Introduce one of your favorite sitcoms to the class.

(2) Watch some video clips from *Home with Kids* and narrate the story in the episode you have watched.

(3) Search for the related materials and present your views on why *Old Uncle and His Sons and Grandsons* and *In-Laws, Out-Laws* were a breath of fresh air to the audience. What special features do these two sitcoms have?

（4）中国大陆受欢迎的情景喜剧《武林外传》却没能在其他华人地区（如中国香港、新加坡）受到欢迎，请跟同学讨论一下，情景喜剧要在某地成功，需要哪些条件？

（5）你认为应该如何区分影视作品的"致敬""模仿""恶搞""抄袭"和"借鉴"？

6. 自我评估

	☺	😐	☹
（1）我能说出情景喜剧的含义和特点。			
（2）我能向别人介绍中国情景喜剧的发展过程。			
（3）我能分析影视作品中采用了哪些致敬、借鉴等艺术手法。			

(4) *My Own Swordsman* is very popular in Chinese mainland. But it is not the same case in Chinese communities in other regions such as Hong Kong SAR and Singapore. Discuss with your classmates what the factors contributing to the success of a sitcom are.

(5) How do you think people should distinguish "showing respect", "imitating", "making a spoof", "plagiarizing", and "learning from others" of film and television works?

6. Self-assessment

	☺	😐	☹
(1) I can tell what sitcom means and list its features.			
(2) I can introduce how sitcoms developed in China.			
(3) I can identify what artistic methods are applied such as "showing respect" and "learning from others" in film and television works.			

1. 学习目标

（1）能说明勾股定理的中国证明方法。

（2）能解答鸡兔同笼类的数学问题。

（3）能说明贾宪三角。

2. 热身活动

讨论

（1）什么是"毕达哥拉斯定理"？中国人怎么称呼这个定理？

（2）勾股定理最早是什么时候被发现的？

（3）有若干只鸡兔同在一个笼子里。从上面数，有35个头；从下面数，有94只脚。笼中各有多少只鸡和兔？如何快速解答这道题？

（4）中国人把1、2、3……这样的数字称为"阿拉伯数字"，这些"阿拉伯数字"是阿拉伯人发明的吗？为什么这样说？

Lesson Three Mathematics in Ancient China

1. Learning objectives

(1) Be able to illustrate the Chinese proof for the Gougu theorem.

(2) Be able to solve the mathematical problem of chickens and rabbits in one cage.

(3) Be able to illustrate Jia Xian Triangle.

2. Warm-up

Discussion

(1) What is the Pythagorean theorem? What do the Chinese call it?

(2) When was the Gougu theorem first discovered?

(3) Some chickens and rabbits are in one cage. There are 35 heads and 94 feet in total. How many chickens and rabbits are there in the cage? How to solve this problem quickly?

(4) Chinese people refer to numbers such as 1, 2, 3 as "Arabic numerals". Were these numerals really invented by Arabs? Why are they called Arabic numerals?

3. 阅读课文

勾 股 定 理

　　勾股定理是一个基本的几何定理，指直角三角形的两条直角边的平方和等于斜边的平方。因为中国古代将直角三角形称作勾股形，较短的直边叫作勾，较长的直边叫作股，斜边叫作弦，所以称这个定理为勾股定理。勾股定理被称作"几何学的基石"，是人类最早发现并证明的重要数学原理之一。中国是发现和研究勾股定理最古老的国家之一。商朝时期的数学家商高提出了"勾三股四弦五"的勾股定理特例，所以这个定理也叫作"商高定理"。后来在公元前6世纪，古希腊著名数学家毕达哥斯拉发现并证明了这个定理，因此世界上许多国家都称"勾股定理"为"毕达哥斯拉定理"。

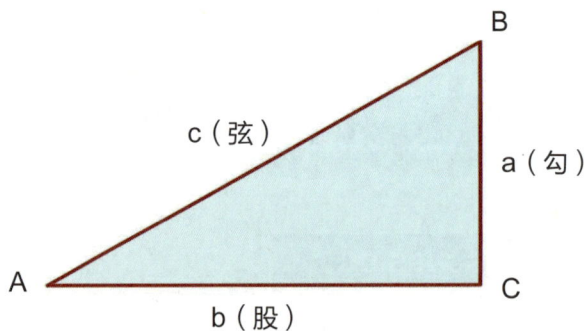

勾股定理中西证明法

　　关于勾股定理的证明方法已经有五百多种，其中中国古代数学家赵爽和美国第20任总统加菲尔德的证明方法非常有名。下面我们一起来了解一下这两种

3. Reading texts

The Gougu Theorem

The Gougu theorem is a basic geometric theorem. It states that in a right triangle, the sum of the squares of the lengths of the legs (a, b) is equal to the square of the length of the hypotenuse (c). In ancient China, the shape of a right triangle had another name, "Gougu", and its short leg was called "gou", long leg "gu", and hypotenuse "xian", which might explain how the theorem got its name. Regarded as the "cornerstone of geometry", the Gougu theorem is one of the most important mathematical rules that humans first discovered and proved. China is one of the ancient countries that discovered and studied this theorem. This theorem is alternatively known as the "Shang Gao theorem" because Shang Gao, a mathematician in Shang Dynasty put forward a typical example for the Gougu theorem: Given Gou (a) was 3, Gu (b) was 4, then Xian (c) was 5.

Later in the 6th B.C., Pythagoras, a famous Greek mathematician, also discovered and proved this theorem. Hence, the "Gougu theorem" is called the "Pythagoras theorem" in many countries around the world.

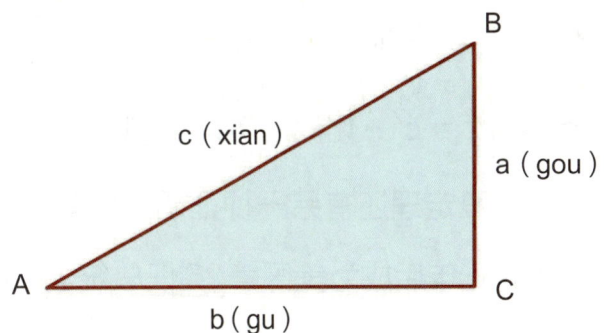

Proofs for the Gougu Theorem both in China and the West

There are over five hundred proofs for the Gougu theorem, among which the proof by Zhao Shuang, a mathematician in ancient China, and that by James A. Garfield, the 20th President of the USA, are well-known. Let's learn about them

不同的证明方法吧。

《周髀算经》中给出的《勾股圆方图注》一开始就说"勾股各自乘，并之为弦实，开方除之，即弦"。实际上这句话给出了两个公式：

（1）勾×勾＋股×股＝弦×弦，也就是 $a^2 + b^2 = c^2$

（2）弦＝$\sqrt{勾^2 + 股^2}$，也就是 $c = \sqrt{a^2 + b^2}$

接着赵爽用一个弦图（见右图）对上面两个公式进行了证明。在这幅"勾股圆方图"中，以弦为边长得到正方形ABDE是由4个相等的直角三角形再加上中间的那个小正方形组成的。每个直角三角形的面积为 $\frac{1}{2}ab$；中间的小正方形边长为b−a，则面积为（b−a）^{2}。于是便可得到下面的式子：$4 \times (\frac{1}{2}ab) +$ （b−a）$^2 = c^2$；化简后可以得到：$a^2 + b^2 = c^2$，也就是：$c = \sqrt{a^2 + b^2}$。

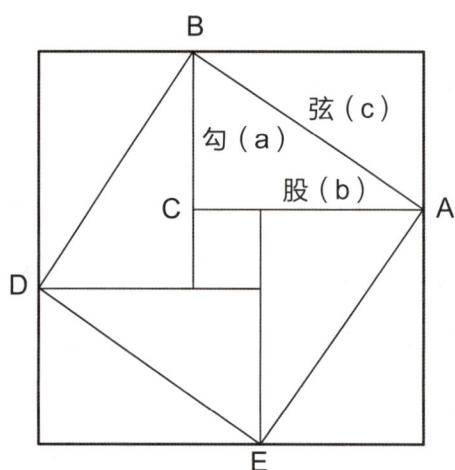

勾股定理还有另一种证明方法叫作"总统证法"，因为加菲尔德在证明勾股定理的五年后成为美国第20任总统。他的证法如下：

as follows:

In the very beginning of the passage "Gougu Yuan Fang Tu Zhu" ("Illustrated Commentary on the Right-Angled Triangle, Circle and Square") in the book *Zhoubi Suanjing*, it is said that "Gōugǔ gèzì chéng, bìngzhī wéi xiánshí, kāifāng chúzhī, jí xián", which actually involves two formulas as follows:

(1) gou (short right side) × gou (short right side) + gu (long right side) × gu (long right side) = xian (hypotenuse) × xian (hypotenuse), that is, $a^2 + b^2 = c^2$

(2) xian (hypotenuse) = $c = \sqrt{a^2 + b^2}$

Zhao Shuang used a figure of hypotenuse (shown on the right) to illustrate the proof of the above two formulas. In this figure, the square ABDE is made up of a small square in the middle and four congruent right triangles, whose hypotenuses are the sides of the square. The area of each right triangle is $\frac{1}{2}$ab. The length of the edge of the small square in the middle is "b−a", then its area is $(b-a)^2$. So we can get a formula: $4 \times (\frac{1}{2}ab) + (b-a)^2 = c^2$, from which we can get a simplified one: $a^2 + b^2 = c^2$, that is, $c = \sqrt{a^2 + b^2}$.

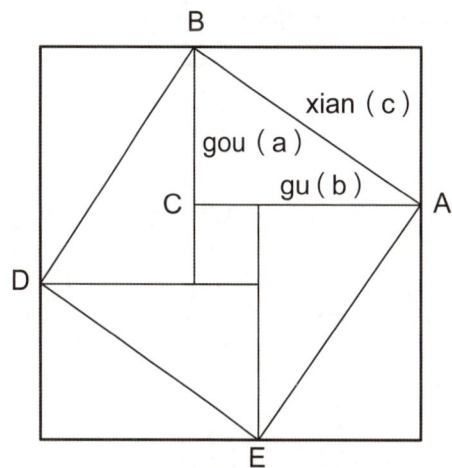

Another proof of the Gougu theorem is called the President Proof, named after James A. Garfield, who became the 20th President of the USA five years after he proved the Gougu theorem.

His proof is illustrated as follows:

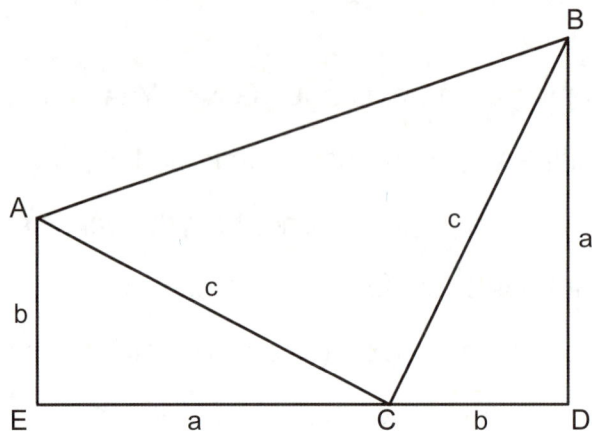

ABDE是直角梯形，面积 $= \dfrac{1}{2}(a+b) \times (a+b) = \dfrac{1}{2}(a+b)^2$，则三角形ACE面积 $= \dfrac{1}{2}ab$

三角形BDC面积 $= \dfrac{1}{2}ab$，三角形ABC面积 $= \dfrac{1}{2}c^2$

所以梯形ABDE面积 $= \dfrac{1}{2}ab + \dfrac{1}{2}ab + \dfrac{1}{2}c^2 = \dfrac{1}{2}(2ab+c^2)$

所以 $\dfrac{1}{2}(a+b)^2 = \dfrac{1}{2}(2ab+c^2)$，$(a+b)^2 = 2ab+c^2$，$a^2+b^2+2ab = 2ab+c^2$

所以 $a^2+b^2 = c^2$

加菲尔德的这种证明方法非常简单、易懂。

鸡 兔 同 笼

鸡兔同笼是中国古代著名的典型趣味题目之一，大约在1,500年前，《孙子算经》中就记载了这个问题，书中是这样说的："今有雉兔同笼，上有三十五头，下有九十四足，问雉兔各几何？"这句话的意思是：有很多鸡和兔子关在

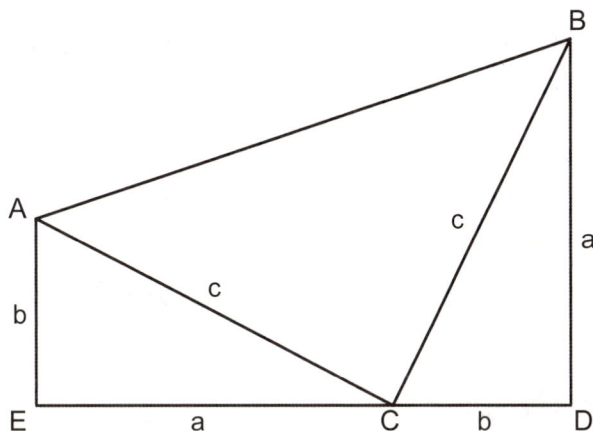

The area of the right-angled trapezoid is $\frac{1}{2}(a + b) \times (a + b) = \frac{1}{2}(a + b)^2$ and the areas of the triangle ACE, BDC, and ABC are $\frac{1}{2}ab$, $\frac{1}{2}ab$, and $\frac{1}{2}c^2$ respectively.

So, the area of the trapezoid ABDE is $\frac{1}{2}ab + \frac{1}{2}ab + \frac{1}{2}c^2 = \frac{1}{2}(2ab + c^2)$.

Hence,

$$\frac{1}{2}(a + b)^2 = \frac{1}{2}(2ab + c^2), \quad (a + b)^2 = 2ab + c^2, \quad a^2 + b^2 + 2ab = 2ab + c^2$$

Therefore, $a^2 + b^2 = c^2$

Garfield's proof of the Gougu theorem is very simple and easy to understand.

Chickens and Rabbits in One Cage

The problem of chickens and rabbits in one cage is one of the most famous interesting mathematical problems in ancient China. Quoted from *Sunzi Suanjing* (*The Mathematical Classic of Master Sun*), written 1,500 years ago, is the sentence "Jīn yǒu zhì tù tónglóng, shàng yǒu sānshíwǔ tóu, xià yǒu jiǔshísì zú, wèn zhì tù gè jǐ hé?" which means "if there are 35 heads and 94 feet visible in a cage housing

同一个笼子里，从上面数有35个头，从下面数有94只脚。问笼中各有多少只鸡和兔？

鸡兔同笼问题有一个很简单的算法，那就是：

（总脚数－总头数 × 鸡的脚数）÷（兔的脚数－鸡的脚数）＝兔的只数

所以上面这道题的解法是：

兔子数 ＝（94－35×2）÷2 ＝ 12（只）

鸡数 ＝ 总头数－兔子数 ＝ 35－12 ＝ 23（只）

这个解法就是假设让兔子和鸡同时抬起2只脚，这样笼子里的脚就减少了总头数（35）×2只，由于一只鸡只有2只脚，所以笼子里只剩下兔子的脚，再除以2就是兔子的数量，最后用总头数减去兔子的数量就是鸡的数量。

贾 宪 三 角

我们都学过多项式乘以多项式，比如：

$(a + b)^0 = 1$

$(a + b)^1 = a + b$

$(a + b)^2 = a^2 + 2ab + b^2$

both chickens and rabbits, how many chickens and rabbits are there?"

To solve this problem, we can use a rather simple equation as follows:

(The number of feet in total − the number of heads in total × the number of chickens' feet) ÷ (the number of rabbits' feet − the number of chickens' feet) = the number of rabbits

Therefore, the above-mentioned problem is solved as follows:

(94 − 35 × 2) ÷ 2 = 12 (the number of rabbits)
35 − 12 = 23 (the number of chickens)

That is to suppose each animal in the cage, be it chicken or rabbit, raises two of its feet. The total number of feet visible in the cage is reduced by 35 (the number of head in total) × 2. Since every chiken has only two feet, now only the rabbits' feet are visible. Divide the number of these feet seen by 2 and you will get the number of the rabbits. Then, the number of chickens is calculated when the number of rabbits is subtracted from the total number of heads.

Jia Xian Triangle

We've probably studied how polynomials are multiplied by other polynomials. For example:

$(a + b)^0 = 1$

$(a + b)^1 = a + b$

$(a + b)^2 = a^2 + 2ab + b^2$

$$(a + b)^3 = a^3 + 3a^2b + 3ab^2 + b^3$$

$$(a + b)^4 = a^4 + 4a^3b + 6a^2b^2 + 4ab^3 + b^4$$

如果我们仔细观察等式右边的系数，就会发现以下规律：

```
            1                n=0
          1   1              n=1
        1   2   1            n=2
      1   3   3   1          n=3
    1   4   6   4   1        n=4
  1   5  10  10   5   1      n=5
1   6  15  20  15   6   1    n=6
```

这些系数的规律在11世纪就被中国数学家贾宪发现了。中国数学界把上面的三角图形称为"贾宪三角"，可以利用它进行高次乘方运算。由于该规则被记载于南宋数学家杨辉所著的《详解九章算法》书中，所以也被叫作"杨辉三角"。

贾宪三角就是二项式系数在三角形中的一种几何排列。这组排列形状为三角形的数字有很多规律，比如：

（1）这个三角形两条斜的边都是由1组成。

（2）每个数等于它上面两个数字之和。

（3）每行数字左右对称，由1开始逐渐变大。

$$(a + b)^3 = a^3 + 3a^2b + 3ab^2 + b^3$$

$$(a + b)^4 = a^4 + 4a^3b + 6a^2b^2 + 4ab^3 + b^4$$

If we observe the above equations carefully, we will find out the rules about the exponents on the right illustrated as follows:

```
              1                    n=0
            1   1                  n=1
          1   2   1                n=2
        1   3   3   1              n=3
      1   4   6   4   1            n=4
    1   5  10  10   5   1          n=5
  1   6  15  20  15   6   1        n=6
```

Such rules about the exponents were discovered in the 11th century by Jia Xian, a Chinese mathematician. The above triangle-shaped diagram is called Jia Xian Triangle, which could be used to extract roots with large exponents. These rules were also recorded in *Xiang Jie Jiu Zhang Suan Fa* written by Yang Hui, a mathematician in the Southern Song Dynasty. Therefore, Jia Xian Triangle is also called Yang Hui Triangle.

Jia Xian Triangle is a triangular array of the binomial coefficients which has many patterns. For example:

(1) The two oblique sides of this triangular array are composed of the number "1".

(2) Each number in this triangular array equals the sum of the two numbers above.

(3) In each row of this triangular array, the numbers are symmetrical along its central column with the smallest number "1" on both sides.

（4）第n行的数字有n项。

（5）第n行数字和为2n － 1。

如果按照这个规律，这个数字三角形可以写到任意层。

这样一种（a＋b）^{n}的展开式中各项系数的规律，在西方数学史上被称为"帕斯卡三角形"，是由法国数学家帕斯卡在1654年所写的书中提出的。

贾宪三角比西方数学界早约600年提出，是中国数学史上的一个伟大成就。

4. 重点词汇

勾股定理

勾股定理指的是什么？

鸡兔同笼

鸡兔同笼问题的简单算法是什么？

贾宪三角

在你们国家，**贾宪三角**有什么别的名称吗？

(4) In this triangular array, there are "n" elements in the line of "n".

(5) In this triangular array, the sum of all the numbers in the line of "n" is "$2n-1$".

You could array this triangular to any size you want if you follow the rule of Jia Xian Triangle.

Such a rule about the terms in the expanded equation of $(a + b)^n$ is called Pascal's Triangle in the Western history of mathematics, which was put forward by Pascal, a French mathematician, in a book he wrote in 1654.

Jia Xian Triangle was put forward about 600 years earlier than that by the Western mathematics community, which could be considered as a great achievement in the history of Chinese mathematics.

4. Keywords

the Gougu theorem/the Pythagorean theorem

What is **the Gougu theorem/the Pythagorean theorem**?

chickens and rabbits in one cage

What is the simple way to solve the problem of **chickens and rabbits in one cage**?

Jia Xian Triangle

Does **Jia Xian Triangle** also have other names in your country?

5. 实践活动

（1）勾股定理除了课文中提到的两种证明方法，还有别的证明方法吗？如果有，请向同学展示。

（2）运用鸡兔同笼的算法，计算下面这道题目：蜘蛛有8条腿，蜻蜓有6条腿和2对翅膀，蝉有6条腿和1对翅膀。这三种小虫共18只，有118条腿和20对翅膀。每种小虫各几只？

（3）除了贾宪，你还知道哪些中国的数学家？你知道他们的成就吗？请小组合作，简单做个报告。

6. 自我评估

	😊	😐	😞
（1）我能说明勾股定理的中西证明法。			
（2）我会计算鸡兔同笼问题。			
（3）我能说明贾宪三角及其规律。			

5. Activities

(1) Are there other proofs of the Gougu theorem, besides the ones mentioned in the texts? If yes, present them to your classmates.

(2) Solve the following problem with the mathematic method of chickens and rabbits in one cage: A spider has 8 legs, a dragonfly has 6 legs and 2 pairs of wings, and a cicada has 6 legs and 1 pair of wings. Given these three kinds of insects are 18 in total, with 118 legs and 20 pairs of wings. How many each kind are there?

(3) Do you know other Chinese mathematicians in addition to Jia Xian? What are their achievements? Work in groups and make a report to the class.

6. Self-assessment

	☺	😐	☹
(1) I can illustrate both Chinese and Western proofs for the Gougu theorem.			
(2) I can solve the problem of chickens and rabbits in one cage.			
(3) I can illustrate Jai Xian Triangle and its rules.			

第四课　地铁

1. 学习目标

（1）能说明中国地铁建设的情况。

（2）能说明地铁给中国城市发展和人们生活带来的便利和不足。

（3）能说明地铁修建中的争论。

（4）了解中国地铁相关制造业的发展。

2. 热身活动

讨论

（1）你坐过中国地铁吗？谈谈你的印象。

（2）坐地铁的时候，你常常做什么？你周围的人呢？

（3）你经常乘坐地铁吗？请说一下坐地铁的优点和不足。

（4）地铁的购票方式有哪几种？它们各有什么便利之处？

（5）中国城市的轨道交通分"地铁"和"轻轨"两种，它们有什么异同？

Lesson Four   Metro System

1. Learning objectives

(1) Be able to discuss the construction of metro systems in China.

(2) Be able to tell the benefits and disadvantages of metro systems for China's urban development and people's life.

(3) Be able to talk about the controversy over the construction of metro systems.

(4) Be able to understand the development of the metro system-related manufacturing industry in China.

2. Warm-up

Discussions

(1) Have you taken the subway in China? What's your impression?

(2) What do you usually do on the subway? How about other passengers around you?

(3) Do you often take the subway? Talk about its advantages and disadvantages.

(4) How many ways of purchasing metro tickets are available? What conveniences does each of them have?

(5) Subway and light rail are the two kinds of rail transport system in Chinese cities. What are their similarities and differences?

（6）中国地铁有的用"subway"，有的用"metro"，研究一下中国不同的城市为什么会用不一样的英语译名。

3. 阅读课文

中国地铁的发展历史

地铁是主要的城市交通工具之一，被称为"绿色交通"。伴随着城市的发展，城市交通压力急剧上升，为了追求高效、通畅、环保的出行方式，中国的各大城市都把地铁作为城市基础设施建设的重要项目，到2017年12月，中国已经有35个城市拥有地铁。

中国的地铁建设始于20世纪50年代的北京。1953年，北京市首次提出修建地铁，得到了国家的支持，在苏联专家的帮助下，我国的技术人员进行了详尽的勘察、设计，确定了地铁的施工方案。但是当时中国的经济发展水平比较落后，地铁建设不得不暂时搁置。一直到1965年，中国才有能力开始建造地铁。那年7月1日，北京开始正式修建中国大陆的第一条地铁，第一期工程全长12公里，于1969年10月1日通车运行，结束了中国大陆没有地铁的历史，也为之

(6) In China, the Chinese term "地铁 (dìtiě)" is translated both as "subway" and "metro". Explore the reasons why different translation versions are used in different cities.

3. Reading texts

The Development History of Metro System in China

Regarded as Green Transport, the subway has become one of the important means of transportation in a city. The development of a city consequently results in increasing pressure on the urban transportation system. To seek for more efficient, smooth, and environmentally friendly modes of transport, big cities in China have listed the construction of metro system as their key infrastructure construction project. As a result, China has built subways in 35 cities by December 2017.

China began to build its first subway in Beijing in the 1950s. In 1953, Beijing proposed to build a subway, which was supported by the government. With the help of the experts from the Soviet Union, Chinese technicians worked out the construction scheme after careful investigation and design. But China was still quite backward in its economy at that time. Thus, the construction of subway had to be halted. It was not until 1965 that China began to build its first subway. On July 1, 1965, the building of the first subway in Chinese mainland officially kicked off in Beijing and its first phase covered a total mileage of 12 kilometers. This subway was put into operation on October 1, 1969, which meant that Chinese mainland ended its history of having no subways. Moreover, Beijing's experience

后其他城市的地铁建设提供了借鉴。

目前中国乃至世界上里程最长的地铁系统是上海地铁。但是上海曾被认为不适合修建地下轨道交通。因为上海临海，土质松软，且含水含沙量大，在这样的地质条件下钻隧道，就像是在"豆腐渣中打洞"，几乎是不可能的。到1990年代，随着盾构技术的应用，上海才开始正式建造地铁。盾构是一种带有护罩的专用设备，施工时，先利用盾构机尾部已装好的衬砌块作为支点向前推进，再用刀盘切割土体，同时排土并拼装后面的预制混凝土衬砌块。在此过程中，壳体也即护盾，对挖掘出的还未衬砌的隧洞起临时支撑的作用，承受周围土层的压力，有时还承受地下水压以及将地下水挡在外面。

地铁建设中的争论

在现代城市发展中，地铁是必不可少的条件。随着中国一批批城市开通地铁，修建地铁已经不再是一二线大城市的专利，一些三线城市也已经开通或者计划开通地铁线路。"地铁一响，黄金万两"，形容的是地铁对城市经济发展的带动作用。不过，修建地铁是一项"烧钱"的工程，中国政府2018年7月13日

is a good lesson that other cities could learn from in constructing their own subways.

Currently, the metro system in Shanghai covers the longest mileage in China and even around the world. Actually, it was once predicted that it was not feasible to build subways in Shanghai, as Shanghai is a coastal city with soft and sandy soil with high soil moisture content. To dig a tunnel under such geological conditions is just like making a hole in soybean curb residues, which sounds impossible to implement. However, when the shield tunneling technology began to be applied, the construction of subways officially kicked off in Shanghai in 1990s. A tunnel boring machine (TBM) is a piece of professional equipment with a protective structure. When operated, the equipment moves forward making use of the lining blocks installed at the back as a fulcrum. Then, the soil is cut by the cutter head and discharged. At the same time, the pre-cast concrete lining block is assembled. In this process, the shield temporarily supports the excavated unlined tunnel to withstand the pressure of the surrounding soil, and sometimes even withstand the pressure from the groundwater and blocking out the water.

Controversy Over the Construction of Metro System

The metro system is essential to the development of a modern city. As subways have been put into operation in many cities, building subways is no longer a privilege exclusive to the first- or second-tier cities. Even the third-tier cities have either started or planned to construct their metro systems. The idiom "as soon as the subway runs, ten thousand ounces of gold comes" gives a vivid description of the impetus of the metro system to the economic

提高了申报建设地铁和轻轨的相关经济指标，要求报建地铁的城市一般公共财政预算收入应在300亿元以上，地区生产总值在3,000亿元以上，市区常住人口在300万人以上；申报建设轻轨的城市一般公共财政预算收入应在150亿元以上，地区生产总值在1,500亿元以上，市区常住人口在150万人以上。

之所以提出这样的要求，是因为地铁建设成本和运营成本都很高。如果一个城市没有很大的客流量，不仅建设的时候是在赔钱，运营的时候也会赔钱。这会给城市财政带来很大的压力。

影响地铁修建的因素除了经济因素，还有其他因素。比如济南市，人口众多，中心城区和繁华地段的交通不堪重负，急需修建地铁降低交通压力，以促进城市的进一步发展。但济南是中国有名的"泉城"，有大大小小泉水七百多处。要在济南修建地铁，最大的挑战就是如何保护好地下泉水。为此，济南修建地铁的事情一拖再拖，直到2015年，经过各方的讨论、研究、实验、技术改进，在保证修建地铁不会影响地下泉水的情况下，济南的第一条地铁线才开始修建，到2019年通车。

development of a city. However, building a subway is a "money-burning" project. On July 13, 2018, the Chinese government raised the relevant thresholds for cities to qualify for new subway and light rail projects. Only cities with more than 3 million permanent residents and that generate more than 30 billion yuan in fiscal revenue and 300 billion yuan in regional GDP are eligible to apply for new subway projects. For light rail projects, cities must have more than 15 billion yuan of fiscal revenue and 150 billion yuan of regional GDP, with more than 1.5 million permanent residents.

Such strict requirements are explained by high construction and operation costs of subways. In case the city does not have a big flow of passengers, both the construction loans and operation deficits of the subways will aggravate the fiscal burden of the city.

Besides financial condition, other factors decide the feasibility of constructing metro system. For example, Jinan is densely populated and its downtown and busy areas are overburdened with heavy traffic. To reduce its traffic burden and further the development of the city, Jinan needs to reconstruct its traffic system. But as a well-known Spring City in China, Jinan has more than 700 springs, big or small. The biggest challenge in building a subway in Jinan is how to protect underground springs. Hence, its construction of the subway system had been put off for quite a long time. It was until 2015 when Jinan started the construction of its first subway line, which was finally put into operation in 2019 after discussions with different sides, research, experiments, and technical improvements guaranteeing that the construction would not affect the underground springs.

国产盾构机

　　中国的城市轨道交通建设离不开关键的设备——盾构机。盾构机又称隧道掘进机，用它进行隧洞施工具有自动化程度高、节省人力、施工速度快、一次成洞、不受气候影响、开挖时可控制地面沉降、减少对地面建筑物的影响和在水下开挖时不影响地面交通等特点，享有"工程机械之王"的美称。

　　以前，中国盾构机技术不成熟，只能从德国或日本进口，价格往往要数亿人民币一台。由于中国基础建设中对盾构机的需求十分巨大，因此科研人员决定自主研究，掌握盾构机的核心技术。经过科研人员的不懈努力，目前中国已经能够建造完全自主研发、直径达15.03米的盾构机，性能达到国外先进水平，价格比国外同类产品低很多。

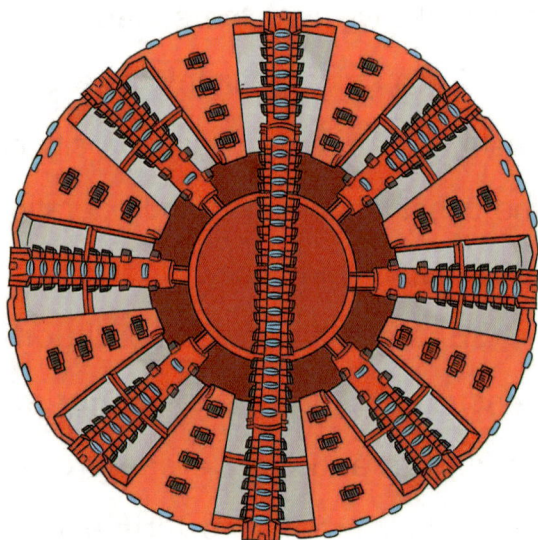

Domestically-Made Shield Tunneling Machine

The construction of rail transport systems in Chinese cities couldn't be possible without a piece of critical equipment, the shield tunneling machine. The shield tunneling machine is also called tunnel boring machine (TBM). TBM is renowned as "King of Construction Machinery", as the highly automated tunneling equipment is both time and labor efficient, and in addition, suitable for all-weather excavation. Furthermore, shield tunneling helps to reduce the risk of ground subsidence, and has little impact on buildings above the ground or waterborne transport in underwater projects.

Years ago, China's technology of shield tunneling machines was not mature. It had to import shield tunneling machines from Germany or Japan at the high price of several hundred million yuan per unit. Since there was a huge demand for shield tunneling machines in the infrastructure construction in China, the scientific research personnel were determined to make research independently and master the core technologies of shield tunneling machines. After the persistent efforts of the scientific research personnel, at present, China is able to independently build its own shield tunneling machine with a diameter of 15.03 meters. Its performance has researched the advanced level in foreign countries while its price is much lower than that of similar foreign products.

如今，中国的盾构机不仅占领了大部分国内市场，而且出口到马来西亚、新加坡等多个国家。中国盾构机因技术先进、价格低廉受到许多国家的青睐。

4. 重点词汇

地铁

地铁建设为什么要花很长时间？

运营

中国的第一条地铁是哪年**运营**的？

盾构机

为了研发**盾构机**，中国的科研人员做了哪些努力？

轻轨　预算

要建设**轻轨**的话，城市财政**预算**需要达到多少？

5. 实践活动

（1）你们国家有没有地铁或者路面电车？请列表比较一下它们和中国地铁的异同。

Today, China's shield tunneling machines not only dominate the domestic market, but also are exported to Malaysia, Singapore and other countries. China's shield tunneling machines are favored by many countries because of their advanced technology and low price.

4. Keywords

subway

Why does it take quite a long time to build a **subway**?

put into operation

When was the first subway **put into operation** in China?

shield tunneling machine

What have the Chinese scientific research personnel done to research and develop their own **shield tunneling machine**?

light rail　budget

How large of a financial **budget** is required for a city if it plans to build a **light rail**?

5. Activities

(1) Does your country have subway or trams? Compare them with Chinese ones and list their similarities and differences in a chart.

（2）上网搜索北京、上海的地铁线路分布图，比较它们的异同，并分析地铁线路设置应考虑的因素。

（3）地铁安检一直是人们讨论的热门话题，有人觉得太麻烦了，应该取消；有人觉得为了保障大家安全，应该保留。你觉得呢？

（4）在你们国家，地铁上可以吃东西吗？中国呢？对于地铁上有人饮食的现象，你怎么看？

（5）假设你在地铁公司工作，请制定一套规则，说明乘坐地铁应该注意的事项。

（6）对于地铁建设和运营需要大量资金的问题，你认为怎样才可以帮助地铁盈利？

(2) Search the network of metro lines in Beijing and Shanghai on the Internet, find out their similarities and differences, and analyze what factors should be considered in planning metro lines.

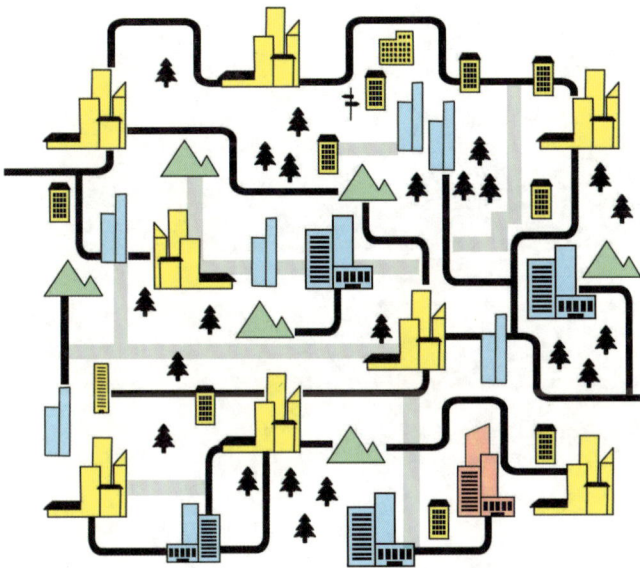

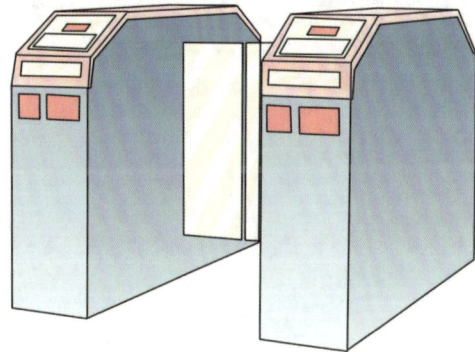

(3) It has been a hot topic whether it is necessary to have subway security check or not. Some think it should be cancelled, as it is too much trouble while others think it should be kept since it ensures people's safety. What's your opinion?

(4) Is it allowed to eat on subways in your country? Is it allowed in China? What do you think when you see someone drinking or eating on subways?

(5) Suppose you worked in a subway company, work out a set of rules and regulations that explain the issues passengers should be aware of when taking subway.

(6) What are your suggestions for subway companies to make profits since the construction and operation of metro system needs a lot of funds?

6. 自我评估

	😊	😐	☹️
（1）我能说明中国地铁的建设情况。			
（2）我能说出地铁对中国城市发展的好处和弊端。			
（3）我了解盾构技术。			
（4）我能说出与地铁相关制造业的发展情况。			

6. Self-assessment

	😊	😐	😞
(1) I can introduce the construction of metro systems in China.			
(2) I can list the advantages and disadvantages the construction of metro systems has brought to the development of Chinese cities.			
(3) I know about shield tunneling technology.			
(4) I can tell how the metro system-related manufacturing industry develops.			

第五课　中国家具

1. 学习目标

（1）能说出中国家具的简单发展历史。

（2）能区分明式家具和清式家具。

（3）能对中外家具风格进行比较。

2. 热身活动

讨论

（1）你看到过中国的传统家具吗？你对这些中国传统家具有什么印象？

（2）请简单说明椅子和凳子在外形和功能上的区别。

Lesson Five　Chinese Furniture

1. Learning objectives

(1) Be able to tell the brief history of Chinese furniture.

(2) Be able to distinguish between furniture of the Ming Dynasty and the Qing Dynasty.

(3) Be able to compare the styles of Chinese furniture with foreign ones.

2. Warm-up

Discussion

(1) Have you seen any traditional Chinese furniture? What impression do you have of it?

(2) Please explain the differences between chairs and stools in shape and function.

（3）从网上找一张中国清代的床的图片，分析一下这种床的特点。

（4）你知道宜家吗？宜家的家具有什么特点？

3. 阅读课文

中国家具发展简史

中国家具随着社会化的进程经历了多层次的变革。

从历史文献可知，中国早在殷商以前就已发明了家具。当时已经有"席""几""扆"（屏风），商代家具还可镶嵌象牙、松石等。

春秋战国时期，生产力水平大有提高，家具的制造水平也有很大提高。当时，像鲁班这样技术高超的工匠不仅促进了家具的发展，而且在木构建筑上也发挥了他们的才能。由于冶金技术的进步，出现了丰富的加工器械和工具，如

(3) Please find a picture of bed of the Qing Dynasty on the Internet and analyze its characteristics.

(4) Do you know IKEA? What are the features of its furniture?

3. Reading texts

A Brief History of Chinese Furniture

Chinese furniture has undergone multi-level changes with social development.

According to historical documents, furniture was invented in China long before the Shang Dynasty. At that time, there were seats, tables, and screens. Furniture of the Shang Dynasty can also be embedded with ivory or turquoise.

During the Spring and Autumn period and the Warring States period, the level of productivity was greatly improved, and so was the manufacturing level of furniture. The emergence of highly skilled craftsmen at that time such as Lu Ban not only promoted the development of furniture, but also gave play to their talents in wooden construction. Due to the progress of metallurgical technology, there

铁制的锯、斧、钻、凿、铲、刨等等，为家具的制造带来了便利条件。相传锯子就是由鲁班发明的，工艺的改进也促进了家具的改进。

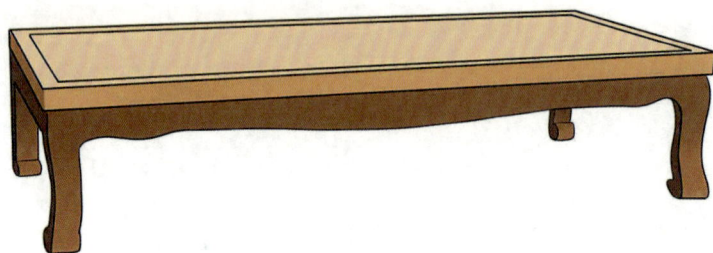

秦汉之前，几、案、衣架和床榻都很矮，都是席地而坐，直到和西域的频繁交流渐深，胡床（一种形如马扎的坐具）开始传入，后来被发展成可折叠马扎、交椅等，为中国的"垂足而坐"奠定了基础。

were abundant processing instruments and tools, such as iron saws, axes, drills, seedlings, shovels, and planers, which brought convenience to the manufacturing of furniture. According to legend, the saw was invented by Lu Ban, and the improvement of technology also promoted the improvement of furniture.

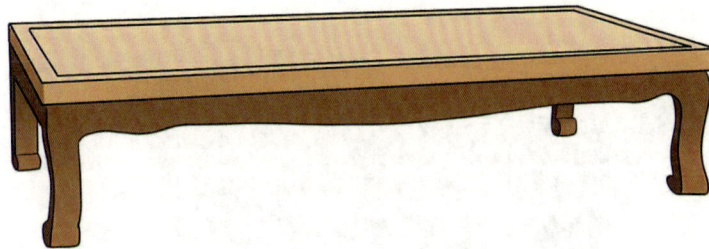

Before the Qin and Han Dynasties, tables, cases, cloth racks, and beds were very short in height, and people usually sat on the ground. Later, when exchange with the Western regions became deeper and more frequent, the Hu bed (a kind of seat shaped like a campstool) began to be introduced, and later it was developed into folding stool, folding chair, and so on. This has laid a foundation for China's "sitting with dropping feet" in later times.

　　西晋起，跪坐的礼节观念渐渐淡薄。至南北朝，垂足坐渐渐流行，出现了一些高形坐具，如墩、椅、凳等，并有笥、簏（箱）等竹藤家具。在装饰方面，漆木家具使用绿沉漆，打破红黑漆的一统格局，同时，由于佛教日兴，家具上出现了莲花纹、忍冬纹、飞天纹。

　　中国家具在唐朝开始变得繁荣。"贞观之治"带来了社会的稳定和文化的空前繁荣。这一时期的家具出现复杂的雕花，并以大漆彩绘，画以花卉图案。 在唐朝的敦煌壁画上，除了可以看到鼓墩、莲花座、藤编墩等，还可以见到形制较为简单的板足案、曲足案、翘头案等。五代画家顾闳中的《韩熙

From the Western Jin Dynasty, the concept of kneeling etiquette gradually became weak. Until the Northern and Southern Dynasties, people preferred to sit with dropping feet, and then the high-form sitting became popular. There emerged some tall furniture like mound, chair and stool, and bamboo plaited suitcases and boxes. In terms of decoration, green sinking lacquer was put into use rather than just traditional red and black lacquer. With the rise of Buddhism, people began to carve patterns like lotus, honeysuckle, or flying Apsaras in their furniture.

The prosperous period of Chinese furniture was in the Tang Dynasty. The governance of Zhenguan brought social stability and unprecedented cultural prosperity. The furniture of this period was intricately carved and painted with large lacquers and floral designs. From the Dunhuang frescoes of the Tang Dynasty, people can not only see the ancient mound, lotus seat, rattan pier, but also see the shape of the relatively simple plate foot case, curved foot case, and

载夜宴图》就是个很好的例子，画面清晰地展示了五代时期家具的使用状况，其中有直背靠背椅、条案、屏风、床、榻、墩等等。唐朝家具完整简洁的形式也预示了明式家具的前期形态，为中国家具在历史上的最完美阶段打下了基础。

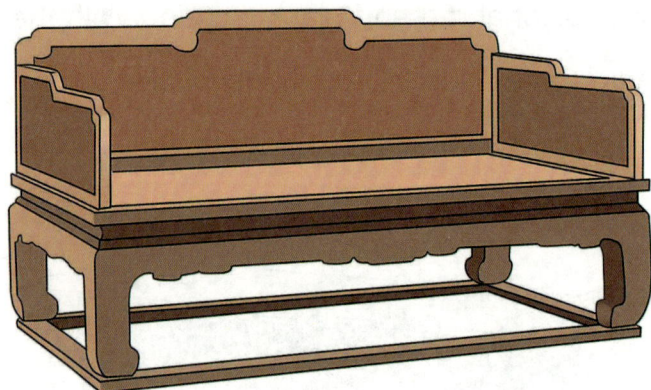

宋朝家具借鉴建筑的梁架结构，使家具结构更趋合理。宋朝家具不作大面积的雕镂装饰，局部点缀以求画龙点睛，与宋人简洁朴素的审美观契合。元朝家具制造者做了两种创造性尝试：一是桌面不探出的方桌，其形象见于冯道真墓壁画，高束腰，桌面不伸出。二是抽屉桌，桌面下设抽屉的创意，以后为明朝所继承，沿用至清。

warped head case. The painting, *Han Xizai Banquet* by Gu Hongzhong, a painter of the Five Dynasties, is a good example. The picture clearly shows the use of furniture in the Five Dynasties, including straight-backed chairs, narrow tables, screens, beds, couches, and so on. The complete and concise form of Tang furniture also foreshadowed the early form of Ming furniture, laying a foundation for the most perfect stage of Chinese furniture in the history.

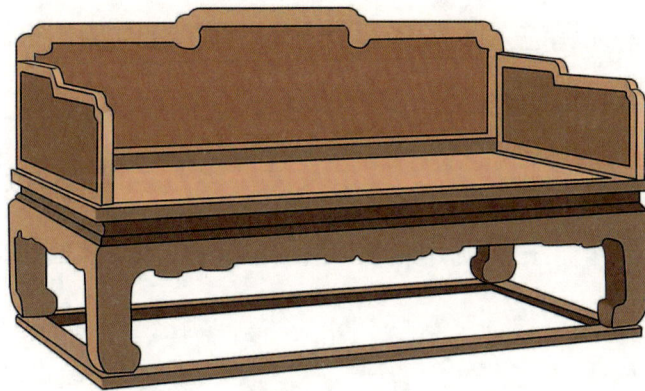

Furniture of the Song Dynasty used the beam-frame structure in architecture to make it more reasonable. Furniture in the Song Dynasty was not carved and decorated in large area, but partly decorated to make the finishing touch, which was in accordance with the simple aesthetic view of the Song people. Furniture makers in the Yuan Dynasty made two creative attempts. One was the square table, which did not protrude from the desktop. Its image could be found in the murals of Feng Daozhen's tomb. It was high with waist and did not protrude from the desktop. The second was the drawer table. The idea of the drawer under the desktop was inherited by the Ming Dynasty and continued to the Qing Dynasty.

　　到了明朝，中国家具进入了完备期，形成了独特风格，被称为"明式家具"。明式家具有四大特点：造型简洁、以线为主；结构严谨、做工精细；装饰适度、繁简相宜；木材坚硬、纹理优美。明式家具历经几百年的变迁，流传至今仍很牢固，除了木材优质外，主要就是榫卯结构的精密和科学合理。

By the Ming Dynasty, Chinese furniture entered a new period, forming a unique style, known as "Ming Furniture". Furniture in the Ming Dynasty has four characteristics: concise shape, line-based; rigorous structure, fine workmanship; moderate decoration, simple, and appropriate; hard wood, graceful texture. After hundreds of years of changes, furniture in the Ming Dynasty is still very strong, owing to not only its high-quality wood, but also the precise and rational tenon-mortise structure.

　　清初家具沿袭明朝风格，用料更为丰盈。除用硬木外，还选用优质软木。乾隆时期，家具生产达到了高峰，装饰手法之多样也史无前例。清式家具的特点主要有：造型上浑厚、庄重；装饰上求多、求满、富贵、华丽。与明式家具的朴素有所不同，它以厚重、繁华、富丽堂皇为标准，给人略有沉闷笨重之感，但也正是由于这种标准，设计者开动脑筋，利用各种手段，巧妙地将不同的元素融入家具，使其受到人们的欢迎。

宜 家 家 居

　　"宜家"是瑞典公司"IKEA"的中文译名，宜家公司于1997年进入中国，2002年在上海开设了第一家标准店。宜家的全部产品由宜家公司设计，强调产品"简约、自然、清新、设计精良"的北欧风格。宜家从创建初期就坚持"提

Furniture in the early Qing Dynasty followed the style of the Ming Dynasty, with more abundant materials. In addition to hardwood, high-quality cork was also used. During the Qianlong period, furniture production reached its peak, and the diversity of decorative techniques was unprecedented. The characteristics of furniture in the Qing Dynasty are as follows: thick and solemn in shape; richness and gorgeousness in decoration. Different from the simplicity of furniture in the Ming Dynasty, furniture in the Qing Dynasty, being heavy, prosperous and magnificent, gave people a slightly dull and heavy feeling. Because of this, designers ingeniously integrated different elements into the furniture by various means to make it unique and popular.

IKEA

"Yijia" is the Chinese translation of the Swedish company IKEA, which entered China in 1997 and opened its first standard store in Shanghai in 2002. All IKEA products are designed by IKEA, emphasizing the Nordic style of "simple, natural, fresh and well-designed" products. IKEA has been adhering to the

供种类繁多、美观实用、老百姓买得起的家居用品"的经营理念，旨在为大量的普通消费者提供价廉物美的家居用品。除了简约的特点之外，宜家家居特别实用，设计很巧妙，尤其是很多产品收纳性特别强，容易搬动和自行拆装，符合了现代中国城市居民的需要，此外，宜家家居所用材料不贵重，价格也在中国居民的可接受范围内。所以虽然在国外，宜家主要受常搬家且住房面积不是很大的年轻人的喜爱，不过在中国，很多中年人也会选择购买宜家家居，甚至把房间布置成"宜家风格"。

宜家公司不仅产品有特色，其服务也值得称道。宜家服务的精细化标准高，工作人员不干扰顾客购物，更不强行推销；宜家的大件商品都是自助选购，样品区标明仓储货架号和位置，顾客到仓储区提货。为配合提货和拿取，仓储区都安排在收银台附近。这种细致的服务不光让顾客感受到了便利，还节省了人力。

4. 重点词汇

家具

你家里的**家具**是中式的还是西式的？

business philosophy of "providing various, beautiful and practical household products that are affordable to ordinary people" since its inception, aiming to provide a large number of ordinary consumers with cheap and fine household products. In addition to its simple features, IKEA furniture is very practical and clever in design. Many of its products are very easy to move and disassemble, which meets the needs of modern Chinese urban residents. In addition, the materials used in IKEA furniture are not expensive and the price is also within the acceptable range of Chinese residents. While IKEA is mainly favored by overseas young people who often move and don't have a large housing area, many middle-aged people in China also choose to buy IKEA furniture and decorate their rooms in the IKEA style.

IKEA has both distinctive products and commendable services. It has a high standard of fine service, and the staff does not interfere with customers' shopping, nor does it force sales. Large goods of IKEA are purchased by self-service. The sample area is marked with storage shelf number and location. Customers pick up goods in the storage area, which is arranged near the checkout counter to make the pick-up more convenient. Such meticulous service not only makes customers feel convenient, but also saves manpower.

4. Keywords

furniture

Is the **furniture** in your home Chinese or Western?

发明

谁**发明**了锯子？

简洁

在挑选家具的时候，你喜欢**简洁**的吗？为什么？

榫卯

什么是**榫卯**结构？

价廉物美

宜家家居为什么可以做到**价廉物美**？

5. 实践活动

（1）明式家具和清式家具都是现在常见的中国古典家具，你更喜欢哪一种家具？为什么？

（2）你去过宜家吗？你喜欢宜家的家具风格吗？为什么？你觉得为什么很多中国人喜欢宜家家具？

（3）探究一下IKEA的中文名字"宜家"有哪些意思。很多在中国的外国公司都会取一个中文名字，你觉得这样做有什么好处？请列举一些外国公司或产品的中文名字，研究一下它们的中文含义。

（4）和你的同学分享自己家里家具的风格，讨论你喜欢什么样的家具以及原因。可以通过拍照等方式让你的分享更为直观。

invent

Who **invented** the saw?

simple

When choosing furniture, do you like the one with a **simple** style? Why?

tenon-mortise structure

What is the **tenon-mortise structure**?

cheap and good

Why is IKEA furniture so **cheap and good**?

5. Activities

(1) Both Ming and Qing Furniture are common classical Chinese furniture. Which do you prefer? Why?

(2) Have you ever been to IKEA? Do you like the style of IKEA furniture? Why? Why do you think many Chinese people like IKEA furniture?

(3) Please find out the meaning of the Chinese name of IKEA. Many foreign companies in China have adopted a Chinese name. What do you think is the advantage of this? Please give more examples of the Chinese names of some foreign companies or products and study their Chinese meanings.

(4) Please share with your classmates the style of the furniture in your home and discuss what kind of furniture you like and why. You can make your sharing more intuitive by taking photos.

（5）以小组为单位，参观上海博物馆的明清家具展览。你对上海博物馆的家具展示中最有印象的是哪一件？为什么它会给你留下最深刻的印象？请与同学们讨论。

6. 自我评估

	:)	:|	:(
（1）我能说出中国家具发展的基本历史。			
（2）我能说出中国明式家具和清式家具的不同之处。			
（3）我能说出中外家具风格的异同。			

(5) In groups, visit the exhibition of Ming and Qing Furniture in Shanghai Museum. Which furniture impresses you the most? Why does it impress you so much? Discuss with your classmates.

6. Self-assessment

	🙂	😐	🙁
(1) I can explain the basic history of the development of Chinese furniture.			
(2) I can tell the differences between Ming and Qing Furniture.			
(3) I can tell the similarities and differences between the styles of Chinese and foreign furniture.			

第六课　中国风音乐

1. 学习目标

（1）能说出中国风音乐的总体特点。

（2）能说出中国风音乐的代表歌曲。

（3）能说出中国风音乐的代表人物及其作品特点。

2. 热身活动

讨论

（1）听《青花瓷》《菊花台》《上海滩》《沧海一声笑》这几首歌曲，然后与同学讨论一下，这几首歌曲在风格上有什么特点？

（2）为什么有些音乐被称为"中国风音乐"？

（3）中国风音乐与西方的摇滚乐等有什么异同？

（4）在你们国家，最受欢迎的歌曲风格有哪些？

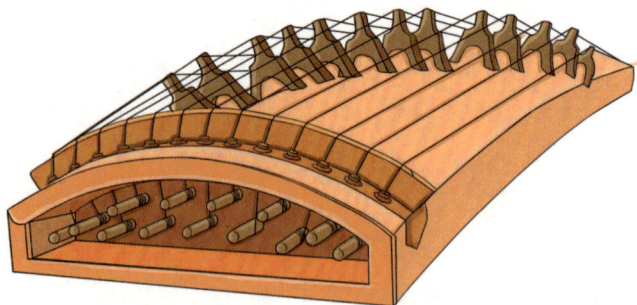

Lesson Six   Chinese-Style Music

1. Learning objectives

(1) Be able to introduce the general features of Chinese-style music.

(2) Be able to name some representative Chinese-style songs.

(3) Be able to introduce several representative Chinese-style musicians and their works.

2. Warm-up

Discussion

(1) Listen to the songs *Blue and White Porcelain*, *Chrysanthemum Terrace*, *Shanghai Bund*, and *A Laughter in the Sea* and then discuss their music styles with your classmates.

(2) Why do people name some music as Chinese-style music?

(3) What are the similarities and differences between Chinese-style music and Western-style music such as Rock and Roll?

(4) What are the most popular music styles in your country?

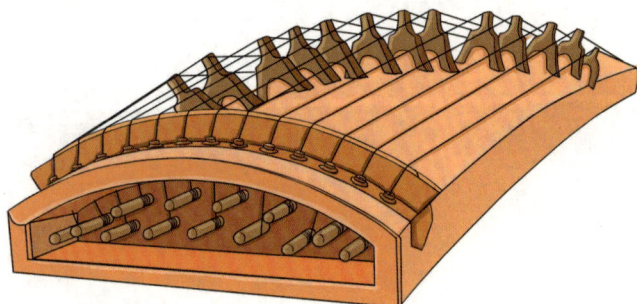

中国风音乐简介

中国风音乐是指三古三新（古诗词、古文化、古旋律、新唱法、新编曲、新概念）结合的中国独特曲风。中国风音乐的歌词具有中国文化内涵，使用新派唱法和编曲技巧烘托歌曲氛围，歌曲以怀旧的中国背景与节奏的结合，产生含蓄、忧愁、轻快等歌曲风格。中国风音乐有一些特点：第一，中国风音乐多采用"宫调式"的主旋律。所谓"宫调式"，就是以宫音为主音的调式。中国古代只分五音，分别是宫、商、角、徵、羽，也就是西方音乐中的"do re mi so la"。第二，中国风音乐在编曲上大量运用中国乐器，如二胡、古筝、箫、琵琶等。第三，演员在歌唱时会运用中国民歌或戏曲方式。此外，中国风音乐的题材多与中国的古诗词或者传说故事有关。

方文山

方文山是中国风歌曲的代表作家。他作的词有很浓重的历史感，内容常常涉及中国古典文化。方文山说自己的歌词是"素颜韵脚诗"。"素颜"是说歌词中都是纯粹的中国文字，没有图片，没有外语单词，也没有数字符号。"韵脚诗"，是指诗歌每行的最后一字押韵，读起来非常顺口，带有流动着的旋律与节奏。

3. Reading texts

Introduction of Chinese-Style Music

Chinese-style music refers to a unique type of music with typical Chinese characteristics, which combines three old elements (ancient poems, ancient cultures, and ancient rhythms) with three new ones (new singing style, new musical arrangements, and new ideas). Lyrics of Chinese-style music have rich connotations in Chinese culture. A new way of singing and composing is applied to set the mood for the song. In such a song, the nostalgic Chinese cultural backgrounds and rhythms are combined to create veiled, blue, and light music. They have some common features. First, Chinese-style music mostly adopts Gong Mode beginning with a Major Scale tone. There were only five tones in ancient China, "Gong", "Shang", "Jue", "Zhi", and "Yu", which correspond to "do re mi so la" in Western music. Second, Chinese musical instrumentals are used in composing Chinese-style music, such as Erhu, Guzheng, Xiao (vertical bamboo flute), and Chinese lute. Third, singing styles of Chinese folk songs or Chinese operas are often adopted. In addition, the themes of Chinese-style music are mostly related to ancient Chinese poetry or legends.

Fang Wenshan (Vincent Fang)

Fang Wenshan is a representative Chinese-style lyricist. His lyrics are created on the basis of history related to Chinese classical culture. Fang Wenshan claims his lyrics as "Su Yan Rhymed Poems". "Su Yan" means that his lyrics are simply Chinese characters without any pictures, foreign words, or numbers. "Rhymed Poems" means that the last character of every line rhymes with each other, which is very readable with a smooth flowing melody and rhythm.

方文山创作了《青花瓷》《菊花台》《东风破》等众多耳熟能详的作品，歌手周杰伦因为演唱他的作品而多次获奖。

黄 霑

黄霑是中国香港地区著名的歌词作者，他写过两千多首非常有名的歌曲，包括《上海滩》《沧海一声笑》《我的中国心》等。他写的词是香港地区流行文化的代表，对香港地区的流行音乐影响巨大。

黄霑作词的歌曲唱起来朗朗上口，不仅带有粤语歌曲独特的音律，还保持其语言文言性的优美。他的词还有很大的一个特色就是运用很多大意象，填词的故事性也非常强。

《上海滩》（节选）

曲：顾嘉辉 词：黄霑

浪奔浪流 万里涛涛江水永不休

淘尽了世间事 混作滔滔一片潮流

是喜是愁 浪里分不清欢笑悲忧

成功失败 浪里看不出有末有

爱你恨你问君知否 似大江一发不收

Fang Wenshan has created many pieces of popular work such as *Blue and White Porcelain*, *Chrysanthemum Terrace*, and *Dong-Feng-Po*. Thanks to his work, the singer Zhou Jielun (Jay Chou) has won many awards.

Huang Zhan (James Wong)

Huang Zhan, a famous lyricist in Hong Kong SAR, China, has written lyrics for more than 2,000 songs, among which *Shanghai Bund*, *A Laughter in the Sea*, and *My Chinese Heart* are the most well-known. His lyrics represent popular culture in Hong Kong SAR and has tremendous impact on its pop music.

The lyrics written by Huang Zhan are quite catchy with the unique musical pattern of Cantonese songs and the beauty of traditional Chinese. His lyrics have another significant feature, that is, he uses a lot of big images and the words themselves tell big stories too.

Shanghai Bund (An Excerpt)

Melody: Gu Jiahui   Lyrics: Huang Zhan

Waves upon waves

For thousands of miles forever flew

Washing the world and its view

In a murky current hitherto

Joy or sorrow

They don't tell which is true

Conquest or foil

转千弯转千滩　　亦未平复此中争斗

又有喜又有愁　　就算分不清欢笑悲忧

仍愿翻百千浪　　在我心中起伏够

爱你恨你问君知否　　似大江一发不收

转千弯转千滩　　亦未平复此中争斗

又有喜又有愁　　就算分不清欢笑悲忧

仍愿翻百千浪　　在我心中起伏够

仍愿翻百千浪　　在我心中起伏够

They don't give even a clue

Say I love you or hate you

Like a river rushing through

Thousands of bends can't subdue

I haven't conquered the strife hereinto

There's joy, there's sorrow

Even if I can't tell which is true

Let hundreds of ebb and flow

Beat me inside to the full

Say I love you or hate you

Like a river rushing through

Thousands of bends can't subdue

I haven't conquered the strife hereinto

There's joy, there's sorrow

Even if I can't tell which is true

Let hundreds of ebb and flow

Beat me inside to the full

Let hundreds of ebb and flow

Beat me inside to the full

港台地区中国风音乐的不同之处

中国台湾地区和香港地区虽然都有中国风音乐，但由于文化、经济制度与历史传承的差别，两地的中国风音乐有着不一样的特征，主要表现在以下几个方面：

第一，整体上来说，台湾地区的中国风音乐比较阳刚，而香港地区的中国风音乐更加阴柔。台湾地区的中国风音乐多以男性的视角叙述，而且以男歌手为主，因此总体呈现出一种阳刚之气。香港地区则正好相反，涉足中国风音乐的，大多是女歌手，选择的视角也是从女性角度出发，显得婉约娇柔。

不过需要指出的是，在2000年前，两个地区的特征正好相反。香港地区的古装剧主题曲以豪迈大气的中国风红遍一时，而八九十年代的台湾地区，民歌运动风风火火，从民歌演变过来的中国风流行曲和以琼瑶为代表的作家从传统诗词改编而来的中国风歌曲，恰恰呈现出一种柔性之美。这其中，最具代表性的就是费玉清演唱的《一剪梅》。

第二，台湾地区的中国风音乐注重意象塑造、文字精雕细琢，而香港地区的中国风音乐则更注重感情的升华。台湾地区的音乐创作人，喜欢把传统文学

Differences Between Lyrics of Chinese-Style Music in Hong Kong SAR and Taiwan Region

Though both music in Taiwan region and Hong Kong SAR are also Chinese-style, they have their own characteristics due to the differences of the culture, economic system, and historical heritage. The differences are illustrated as follows:

Firstly, generally speaking, Chinese-style music in Taiwan region is rather masculine, while that in Hong Kong SAR is more feminine. Works of Chinese-style music in Taiwan region usually tell stories from the male perspective and the singers are mainly males. Hence, they exhibit a spirit of masculinity. In contrast, in Hong Kong SAR, Chinese-style music is mostly sung by female singers and the themes are selected from the perspective of a female, which contributes to its feminine quality.

Nevertheless, the situations in these two regions were just the other way before 2000. At that time, many title songs of costume dramas in Hong Kong SAR became popular overnight by their heroic Chinese style, while in Taiwan region in the 1980s and 1990s, the folk song movement was in full swing. Under such a circumstance in Taiwan region, Chinese pop songs were evolved from folk songs and Chinese-style songs were adapted from the traditional poetry by some writers represented by Qiong Yao. These songs exhibit a kind of gentle beauty. Among them, *A Spray of Plim Blossoms* performed by Fei Yuqing is the most representative.

Secondly, Chinese-style music in Taiwan region gives importance to creation of images and elaborate use of words, while in Hong Kong SAR, emotional

中的一些意象放入歌词内，营造出一种古香古色的特征。同时，台湾地区的中国风音乐注重用古典名词营造美感。香港地区的中国风音乐则更加注重歌词背后的意义以及深远的文化意义，不刻意强调使用古典词汇，甚至在中国风歌词里面，会出现一些现代词汇。

第三，叙述视角有差异。台湾地区的中国风音乐，常常是将主体"我"带入，即"我"是中国风歌词中的主人公，以此为中心创作。把个人带入某个时代中的某一个角色，这些中国风音乐就有了特定的时空年代。香港地区则明显不同，大多数情况下，词人是站在局外，以第三人称的口吻来叙述的，这样的写法，跳出了第一人称的局限，使其在情感的升华上，扩大了空间范围，也让其在创作上，能够多一些类似旁白的自我解说。

4. 重点词汇

中国风

中国风音乐有哪些特点？

韵脚

中国古代诗歌中的**韵脚**是怎么表现的？

expression is given a priority. In Taiwan region, the composers prefer to borrow some images from traditional literary works to give the lyrics a sense of classical beauty. Meanwhile, archaic expressions are used to create a sense of beauty. However, in Hong Kong SAR, Chinese-style music pays more attention to the meaning between the lyrical lines and their profound cultural significance. The use of archaic expressions is not emphasized intentionally. Modern expressions are also used.

Thirdly, the perspectives of narration are different. In Taiwan region, Chinese-style music often adopts a first-person point of view with "I" (the singer) being the protagonist, which gives a sense of particular time and space as the singer assumes a specific identity. In sharp contrast, in Hong Kong SAR, Chinese-style music adopts a third-person point of view in many cases, which gives lyricists advantages of a broader perspective as well as greater freedom for motional expression compared with the first-person point of view. Telling stories as an outsider also has an effect of self-explanation in a voice-over fashion.

4. Keywords

Chinese-style music

What are the features of **Chinese-style music**?

rhyme

How does the **rhyme** manifest itself in ancient Chinese poetry?

歌词

中国香港地区和台湾地区的中国风音乐在**歌词**上有什么差别？

意象

《上海滩》这首歌中有什么**意象**？

5. 实践活动

（1）中国风流行歌曲具体来说是一种什么样的风格？请用自己的语言和同学分享一下。

（2）中国风音乐是外来音乐风格和中国传统音乐风格结合的产物，你认为为什么这种风格会变得流行？请查阅资料，结合中国风流行音乐的发展历史做一下分析。

（3）有人说，中国风流行歌曲在国外认可度不高，你是否同意这样的观点？为什么？

（4）课文中说明了中国台湾地区和香港地区在中国风音乐上的差异，你是否同意？能否找一些例子来说明？除了课文中谈到的几点，你觉得还有哪些差异？

（5）你们国家独特的音乐风格是什么？请找几首代表歌曲和同学分享，并介绍这些音乐的风格特点。

（6）请学唱一首你最感兴趣的中国风歌曲。

lyric

What are the **lyrical** differences between Chinese-style music in Hong Kong SAR and Taiwan region?

image

What **image** does the song *Shanghai Bund* express?

5. Activities

(1) What are the characteristics of Chinese-style pop songs? Share your ideas in your own words with the class.

(2) Chinese-style music is the combined product of foreign music and Chinese traditional music. Why has it become so popular? Look for information and make an analysis based on the history of the development of Chinese-style pop music.

(3) Some people say that Chinese-style pop songs are not recognized abroad. Do you agree with this view? Why or why not?

(4) Illustrated in the text are the differences between Taiwan region and Hong Kong SAR in terms of Chinese-style music. Do you agree with the points? Find more examples to illustrate these differences. Could you find other differences?

(5) What is the unique music style of your country? Find several representative songs, share them with your classmates, and introduce the characteristics of the music style.

(6) Try to learn one Chinese-style song that interests you the most.

6. 自我评估

	🙂	😐	☹️
（1）我能说出中国风音乐的总体特点。			
（2）我能说出中国风音乐的代表歌曲。			
（3）我能说出中国风音乐的代表人物及其作品特点。			

6. Self-assessment

	😊	😐	😠
(1) I can list the general features of Chinese-style music.			
(2) I can name some representative Chinese-style songs.			
(3) I can name some representative musicians of Chinese-style music and the characteristics of their works.			

第七课 禁忌文化

1. 学习目标

（1）能说明中国文化中的数字禁忌。

（2）能说明中国文化中的颜色禁忌。

（3）了解中国人送礼的礼节和注意事项。

（4）了解中国古代的避讳文化。

2. 热身活动

讨论

（1）中国人生活中喜欢什么数字？不喜欢什么数字？为什么？

（2）在你们国家，结婚时新娘一般穿什么颜色的衣服？为什么？中国的新娘常常穿什么颜色的衣服？

（3）你常常送什么礼物给朋友？可以直接送给朋友钱吗？

（4）在中国，哪些东西不能作为礼物送给别人？

（5）你会直接称呼父母名字吗？中国人会这样做吗？

Lesson Seven   Taboo Culture

1. Learning objectives

(1) Be able to explain number taboo in Chinese culture.

(2) Be able to explain color taboo in Chinese culture.

(3) Have some knowledge about the Chinese gift-giving etiquette.

(4) Have some knowledge about the naming taboo culture in ancient China.

2. Warm-up

Discussion

(1) Which numbers are favored by Chinese people in their life? Which are disfavored? Why?

(2) What color does a bride in your country usually wear at her wedding ceremony? Why? What about a bride in China?

(3) What gifts do you usually give to your friends? Would you give them cash as a gift?

(4) What cannot be given as gifts in China?

(5) Do you call your parents by their names? Would Chinese people do this?

3. 阅读课文

数 字 禁 忌

一对夫妇在新西兰奥克兰市区看中了一套房子，因地址里含有数字"4"，华人买家不喜欢，因此房子的价格比较便宜。买家太太回忆，当天拍卖房子时，满屋子都是华裔买家，那些买家对其他房子都竞争激烈，唯独没有人举牌买这套房子。导致这种现象的主要原因是汉语中"4"的发音和"死"很像，中国人很忌讳，所以他们会避开购买地址中含有"4"的房子。

中国人除了忌讳数字"4"，还不喜欢"3"和"7"这样的单数，这样的数字被认为是不吉利的。因为自古以来，中国人就讲究"好事成双"，因此，无论是手机号码还是车牌号，人们都十分喜欢双数，比如"6""8""10"。"6"表示"六六大顺"；"8"与"发"谐音，表示人们希望"发财"的愿望；"10"表示"十全十美"的意思。

3. Reading texts

Number Taboo

A couple took a fancy to a house in the downtown area of Auckland, New Zealand and bought it at a low price. The house was relatively cheap, just because its address contained the number "4", which was disfavored by Chinese buyers. The wife of the buyer recalled that the auction house was full of Chinese buyers on the day it was auctioned. However, they bid competitively for all the other houses except this one. The main reason is that the pronunciation of the number "4" (sì) in Chinese is quite similar to that of "death" (sǐ), which is a taboo to Chinese people. They will avoid buying a house with a "4" in the address.

Just like how the number "4" is a taboo to Chinese, they also don't like some odd numbers such as "3" and "7" , which are considered unlucky. Since ancient times, Chinese people have held the belief "good things come in pairs". That's why people favor even numbers when they choose numbers for their cell phones and license plates, such as "6" , "8" , and "10". "6" means "everything goes smoothly"; "8" (bā) is homonymous with the character "发" (fā) expressing one's wish for good fortunes (发财, fācái); "10" means "being perfect in everything" (十全十美, shíquánshíměi).

颜色禁忌

　　大红色被中国人认为是最吉祥、最喜庆的颜色。逢年过节和喜庆节日都少不了红色，比如在中国古代，婚礼上新娘和新郎都必须穿大红色的衣服、新娘要坐大红花轿、屋里屋外要贴红双喜。另外，除夕之夜，家家户户都要挂大红灯笼、贴春联，表示新的一年红红火火。

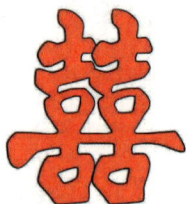

Color Taboo

Chinese people regard red as the most auspicious and festive color. Red is indispensable to festivals and celebrations, including New Year. It is said that in ancient China at a wedding ceremony, both the bride and bridegroom should wear red, the bride should sit in a red Bridal sedan chair, and the phrase "Double Happiness" should be put up somewhere inside and outside of the house in red words. Also, on New Year's Eve, every family and household will hang red lanterns and put up red antithetical couplets to express good wishes for a flourishing new year.

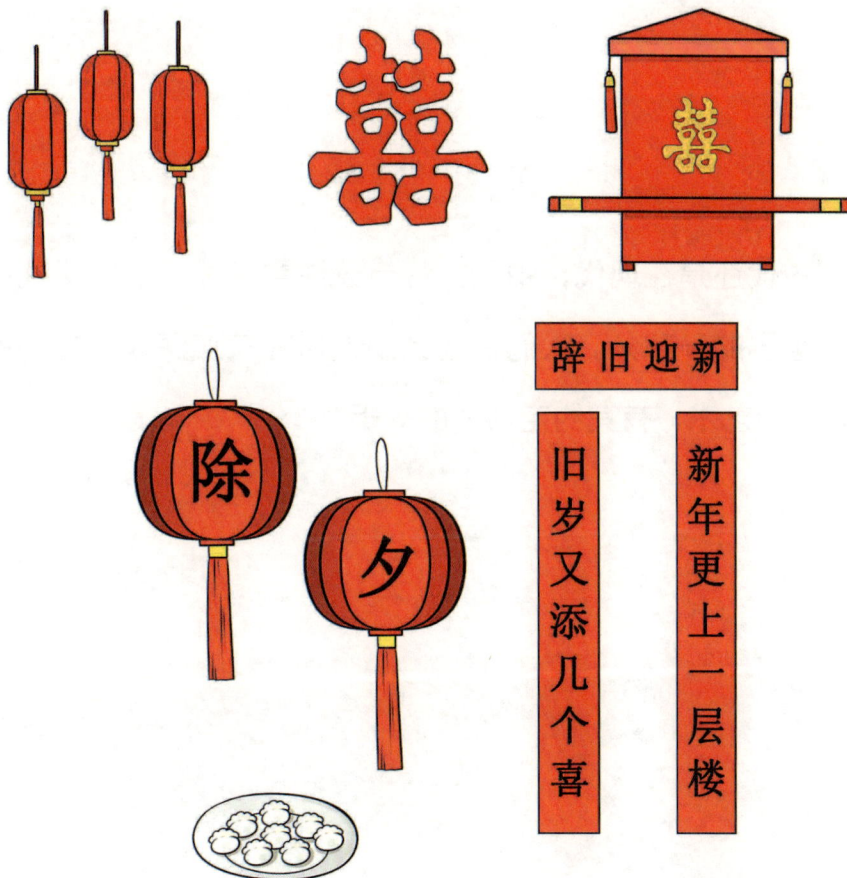

辞旧迎新

旧岁又添几个喜　　新年更上一层楼

　　除此之外，中国人还喜欢黄色。黄色被认为是帝王之色，在古代只有皇帝才可以使用这种颜色，比如故宫的屋顶，还有皇帝的衣服都是黄色的，象征着权威、富贵和大方气派。

　　与之相反，中国人对白色就有些忌讳，因为白色自古以来被认为和死亡有关，只有有人去世的时候，才会用到白色，是不吉利的颜色。

　　不过颜色的这种禁忌也在发生着变化，改革开放以来，中国人受到西方的影响，城市里的女性结婚时，除了准备一套中式的红色结婚礼服，也会穿白色的西式婚纱。城里人在出席葬礼时也往往和西方人一样穿黑色外套，不过在农村或者经济不发达的地区，人们仍然遵守葬礼一定要穿白色衣服和鞋子这样的传统习俗。

送 礼 文 化

　　无论是在古代还是在现代，中国人都十分注重送礼，所以送礼自古以来就是中国文化中重要的一部分。人们往往会通过送礼来加深双方之间的感情。在中国，送礼是一门艺术，有其约定俗成的规矩。

In addition, Chinese people show favor to yellow, which is considered the color of the emperor. In ancient times, only emperors have the privilege of using this color. For example, the roof on the Imperial Palace is yellow and the emperors' robes are yellow. Yellow is a symbol of authority, wealth, elegance, and prestige.

In contrast, there are some taboos against white. Since ancient times white has been associated with death. As an unlucky color, white is only used at funerals.

Nevertheless, taboos against colors vary. Since the implementation of the reform and opening-up policy, Chinese people have been influenced by the Western cultures. In cities, when a girl gets married, she will prepare a white Western-style wedding dress for her wedding ceremony in addition to the red Chinese-style one. People in cities attending a funeral are dressed in black like Westerners. But in countryside and the economically underdeveloped regions, people still strictly follow the traditional customs such as wearing white garments and shoes at funerals.

Etiquettes of Giving Gifts

Whether in ancient times or the modern era, the Chinese always pay high levels of attention to gift-giving etiquette, which has become an important part of Chinese culture. By giving gifts to each other, people strengthen their relationships. Therefore, in China, giving gifts is an art and has its own traditional rules.

　　中国人送礼很讲究礼物的包装。一般认为，精美的包装不仅可以表示你对对方的尊重，而且代表了你对双方之间感情的重视。另外，"要面子"也是中国人讲究包装的原因之一。白色和黑色的包装是送礼的禁忌，因为中国人认为白色和黑色都是不吉利的颜色，会带来灾难。

　　其次，送礼也要考虑双方之间感情的深浅。如果你们之间感情不深，尽量不要送特别贵重的礼物，免得给对方造成压力。而且，中国人还讲究"礼尚往来"。走亲访友时，人们一般会送酒、茶、烟、水果等。但现在，无论是参加婚礼还是逢年过节，人们相互送红包变得越来越普遍。

　　此外，中国人送礼忌讳"钟"，因为"送钟"和"送终"谐音；由于"梨""伞"与"离""散"谐音，表示分开，也是不吉利的，所以不可以送。除此之外，绿色的帽子也是绝对不可以送人的。

How to wrap a gift is taken into careful consideration when the Chinese give gifts. Generally speaking, an elaborately wrapped gift can not only show your respect to others, but also imply that you treasure the friendship. Another reason why the Chinese wrap a gift carefully is that they give much importance to "face saving". In addition, it is a taboo to wrap a gift in white or black, because the Chinese consider these two colors ominous, which will bring people catastrophes.

Secondly, the degree of closeness with a friend should be taken into consideration in giving gifts. Avoid giving a casual friend an expensive gift, otherwise you might give him/her pressure, as the Chinese concept of "reciprocity" requires the friend send you an equally expensive gift in return. When visiting friends and relatives, the Chinese usually take such gifts as wine, tea, cigars, and fruits. Nevertheless, it has now become more and more popular to give "red envelopes" when attending wedding ceremonies and celebrating festivals and holidays.

Furthermore, it is a taboo for the Chinese to give others a clock (zhōng) as a gift because "送钟" (sòngzhōng), which means "giving a clock", is homophonous to "送终" (sòngzhōng), which means "handling the funeral affairs of the senior". Also, it is a taboo to give others a pear (lí) or an umbrella (sǎn) since "梨" (lí) is homophonous to "离" (lí) while "伞" (sǎn) is homophonous to "散" (sàn). Both "离" (lí) and "散" (sàn) express the meaning of "breaking up", which is considered ominous. Besides, it is another taboo to give others a green cap as a gift.

避　讳

　　避讳是中国封建社会特有的现象。它源于古老的语言禁忌，是人们为了对帝王将相、圣贤和长辈表示尊敬，在说话时必须避免直呼其名或者在写文章时直写其名。

　　避讳最常见的三种办法分别是：改字、缺笔和空字。改字指的是将某个字改成另一个字。缺笔是指将字省去一两笔，这个方法大约开始于唐代。人们为了避唐太宗李世民的讳，会将"世"字写成"卅"。空字的意思是为了避讳，将字直接空在那边不写或画以"□"，或用"某"字代替，或直接写"讳"字。例如古代有个叫"王世充"的人，唐代的史书中，为了避李世民的讳，提到王世充时，会将其中的"世"字省去，空在那里不写。

　　在现代社会，尽管上述避讳已经很少使用了，但中国人一般在生活中仍不会直呼父母、长辈和老师的姓名。

Naming Taboo

The naming taboo is peculiar to Chinese feudal society. It originates from the ancient language taboo against speaking or writing given names of exalted people, such as emperors, high-positioned officials, sages, and elders, to show respect to them.

There are three most common ways to avoid using a taboo character: changing the character, omitting strokes, and leaving the character as a blank. The way of changing the character is to replace the character with another one. Beginning from the Tang Dynasty, one or two strokes would be omitted in the character. In order to avoid using a character from the name of Emperor Taizong of Tang, Li Shimin, the character "世" (shì) was written as "卅" (sà). The character could be left blank by either not writing the character, drawing a "□" instead, replacing the character with the character "某" (mǒu), which means "somebody", or writing the character "讳" (huì) instead, which means "taboo". For example, there was a person in ancient times whose name was "王世充" (Wang Shichong). To avoid using a character from the Emperor "李世民" (Li Shimin), the character "世" (shì) is not written and left as a blank.

In the modern society, though the above naming taboo is rarely used, the Chinese will not address their parents, the elders, and teachers by their names.

4. 重点词汇

禁忌

你们国家有哪些数字**禁忌**？

送礼　讲究

中国人**送礼**时**讲究**什么？

谐音

在你们国家，有没有"**谐音**"的文化？

避讳

避讳的主要方法有哪些？

5. 实践活动

（1）分组活动，总结一下不同国家在数字或者颜色方面的禁忌，然后向全班做汇报。

（2）除了课文里介绍的数字和颜色禁忌外，在你们国家还有哪些禁忌？

（3）有人认为禁忌是一种迷信，应该破除。你怎么看这种观点？

（4）如果你的亲戚结婚，一般你们会送什么礼物？问问其他国家的同学，

4. Keywords

taboo

What are the **taboos** against numbers in your country?

give gifts   pay attention to

What etiquettes should the Chinese **pay attention to** when **giving gifts**?

homophonous

Does the language in your country have the phenomenon of **homophonous** words?

naming taboo

What are the main methods of avoiding **naming taboo**?

5. Activities

(1) In groups, summarize taboos against numbers and colors in different countries and then give a report to the class.

(2) Are there any other taboos in your country besides the taboos against numbers and colors introduced in the text?

(3) Some people think taboos are a kind of superstition and should be cast out. What's your opinion?

(4) If one of your relatives gets married, what gifts will you give him/ her? Talk with your classmates from other countries to learn the customs

了解一下他们国家结婚送礼的风俗，分析一下产生这些风俗的原因。

（5）中国人有送红包的习俗。问问中国人，在哪些情境下需要送红包，一般送多少钱？你们国家有没有类似的送红包习俗？

6. 自我评估

	☺	😐	☹
（1）我能说明中国人的数字禁忌。			
（2）我能说明中国人的颜色忌讳。			
（3）我能说出中国人送礼时的注意事项。			
（4）我能说出一些中国人的避讳观念和避讳方法。			

of giving wedding gifts in their countries. Then, analyze why there are such different customs.

(5) The Chinese have the custom of giving "red envelopes". Talk with the Chinese and ask when they usually give others "red envelopes" and how much money they put in it. Is there a similar custom in your country?

6. Self-assessment

	☺	😐	☹
(1) I can exemplify what taboos the Chinese have against numbers.			
(2) I can exemplify what taboos the Chinese have against colors.			
(3) I can list the dos and don'ts when the Chinese give gifts.			
(4) I can talk about the concept of naming taboo the Chinese have and the ways of avoiding using a taboo character.			

第八课　网络文学

1. 学习目标

（1）能说出一些影响广泛的中国网络文学作品的名字。

（2）能说明中国网络文学的发展情况。

（3）能分析影响中国网络文学发展的因素。

2. 热身活动

讨论

（1）你平时喜欢看什么书？为什么喜欢看这些书？

（2）你会上网看小说吗？你认为为什么大家会在网上看小说？

（3）作家有时候在网上写书并没有稿费，那么为什么他们还愿意在网上写书呢？

（4）你觉得什么样的网络文学作品容易受到读者欢迎？

3. 阅读课文

中国网络文学的发展

互联网于20世纪90年代开始在中国流行，它与中国传统文学的相遇，产生了一种文学发展的新模式——网络文学。网络文学不仅方便了读者的阅读，也

Lesson Eight Network Literature

1. Learning objectives

(1) Be able to name some influential Chinese network literary works.

(2) Be able to talk about the development of Chinese network literature.

(3) Be able to analyze the factors affecting the development of Chinese network literature.

2. Warm-up

Discussion

(1) What sort of books do you often read? Why do you like reading these books?

(2) Have you ever read novels online? Why do people like reading novels online?

(3) Why are authors keen to create online literary works even though they are sometimes not paid?

(4) What sort of network literary works are popular with readers?

3. Reading texts

The Development of Chinese Network Literature

The Internet has been popular in China since the 1990s. Its encounter with Chinese traditional literature later created a new model of literature—network

为作者带来了发表作品与传播意见的便利，为作者和读者之间的互动创造了更多的可能。

中国网络文学的起步离不开20世纪80年代中国海外留学生的贡献，互联网为身在异国他乡的学子们的情感表达提供了便利，在网络上抒发情感的文学作品自然应运而生。著名美籍华人作家少君所著小说《奋斗与平等》是目前所知最早的一篇中文网络小说，该文于1991年4月发表于网络，开启了中国网络文学的先河。

然而，海外留学生并非传统意义上的著名作家，而多是文学爱好者和计算机爱好者。他们的写作几乎没有商业利益的驱动，起初也没有大量的读者，而仅凭个人的兴趣和爱好坚持创作。

1997年，美籍华人朱威廉依托其创作的个人主页创办了国内最早、最具品牌的文学类网站——"榕树下"，其特色即是以中国青年倾诉和表达思想、情感为主，并坚持"文学是大众的文学"。之后网络文学进入一个全民写作的时代，越来越多的门户网站也开始为作者提供写作平台，将广大网民聚集起来。许多优秀作品也相继诞生，如赵赶驴（原名聂海洋）所著的《赵赶驴电梯奇遇记》，该文刚发表3个月就创造了1亿次点击量的神话，紧随其后的《鬼吹灯》也突破

literature. Network literature is more convenient not only for readers to read but also for authors to post their works and spread their opinions, providing more possibilities for readers and authors to communicate with each other.

Chinese network literature could not have survived without the contributions from Chinese overseas students in the 1980s. The Internet provides a more convenient emotional outlet for overseas students, hence the birth of network literature. *Struggle and Equality* written by Chinese-American author Shao Jun is the earliest Chinese network literary work that people ever knew. It was published online in April 1991, and became the pioneer of Chinese network literature.

Nevertheless, most of these overseas students are not well-known writers in the traditional sense, but amateurs with enthusiasm for literature and computers. They are barely motivated to write through commercial interests and did not have a large number of readers in the beginning. Instead, they insist on writing simply due to their personal interest.

In 1997, based on his previously personal blogs, a Chinese-American named William Zhu set up Banyan Tree, the earliest domestic literature website. On this unique website, Chinese youths expressed their ideas and poured out their feelings, upholding the principle of mass literature. After that, network literature entered an era of mass writing. Meanwhile, more and more websites began to provide platforms for writers, which successfully attracted many netizens. Many brilliant works then emerged one after another, such as *Adventures of Zhao Ganlv in the Elevator* by Zhao Ganlv whose real name is Nie Haiyang. His work created a marvel of achieving the click-rate of one hundred million only within three months after it was released. Another novel known as

千万点击量。

　　随着互联网的普及，中国网络文学作品不断涌现，而中国网络文学黄金时代开启的标志则是作家蔡智恒（昵称痞子蔡）于1998年所发表的《第一次的亲密接触》，该小说的出现意味着中国网络文学的成熟，并对中国当代网络文学的发展产生了巨大的影响。随后，越来越多的作者开始在网站上连载自己的作品，例如庆山（安妮宝贝）在文学网站"榕树下"发表连载小说《告别薇安》，今何在新浪网的金庸客栈发表《悟空传》等。

　　网络文学在快速发展的同时，也不断与影视、动漫、游戏等产业合作，与市场相结合。如网络作家文雨于2010年创作的《网逝》入选第五届鲁迅文学奖，成为首个入围鲁迅文学奖的网络文学作品，并于2012年更名为《搜索》后改编为同名电影在全国公映。又如《花千骨》《三生三世十里桃花》《琅琊榜》《盗墓笔记》等网络文学作品被改编为影视剧并深受热捧。多元发展模式不断丰富了网络文学的发展平台，为网络文学在21世纪的发展注入了新的生命力。因此，网络文学的发展不是单向发展，而是带动了一整条产业链的发展。

Ghost Blows Out the Candle also achieved the click-rate of more than ten million.

With the popularity of the Internet, many literary works have been springing up. The beginning of the golden age of Chinese network literature was marked by the publication of *First Intimate Contact*. It was written by novelist Cai Zhiheng, nicknamed Pizi Cai ("Ruffian Cai" in meaning). As a symbol of a mature work in Chinese network literature, this novel made a great impact on the development of Chinese contemporary network literature. After that, more and more writers started to upload and serialize their articles online, such as *Goodbye Vivian*, which was posted by Qingshan (also named Annie Baby before) on Banyan Tree, and *Countergod Man*, which was released by Jin He for the column "Jin Yong Kezhan" on Sina.

Accompanied by its rapid development, network literature began to seek its cooperation with some industries such as film, anime, and video game to meet the commercial needs of the market. For instance, the novel *Wang Shi* written by online writer Wen Yu in 2010 was nominated for the fifth Lu Xun Literature Award. It was the first network literary work to be shortlisted for this Award. In 2012, *Wang Shi* changed its name into *Sou Suo* (*Caught in the Web*). Later it was adapted to a film with the same name and released nationwide in China. Other network literary works such as *The Journey of Flowers*, *Eternal Love*, *Nirvana In Fire*, and *Explore with the Note* were also adapted to movies and TV dramas and then became popular in China. Such a development model not only enriches the network literature platforms but also adds new life to the development of network literature in the 21st century. Therefore, network literature doesn't develop by itself, but drives the development of an entire industrial chain.

中国网络文学的快速发展也产生了其他效应，例如许多网络文学作者加入到以网络收费和实体出版为目的的写作队伍中，这导致了网络文学创作的泛滥化和低质量化。当然，这也使网络文学的体裁呈现出多样性和前卫性特征，尤其是玄幻、穿越类题材型小说开始流行，如玄幻小说《诛仙》、穿越小说《梦回大清》等曾一度受到网民读者的热捧。因此，网络文学的分类也不再拘泥于文学、诗歌、小说等传统类型的划分，取而代之的是玄幻、奇幻、穿越、都市、军事，甚至二次元等更为具体、细致的分类。

Furthermore, there are some side effects with the rapid development of Chinese network literature. For example, many online writers began to write for the pay-to-surf websites or intended to get their works published in print, which consequently has led to the proliferation of low-quality online literature. However, at the same time, the genres of network literary works have become more diversified and the avant-garde element has been added. Fantasy and time-travel novels such as *Jade Dynasty* and *A Dream Back to the Qing Dynasty* have become extremely popular with netizens. As a result, the classification of network literary works goes beyond the traditional types which include literary art, poetry, and novels. Instead, they are put into more detailed and subtle categories including fantasy, supernatural narrative, narration of changes in space-time locations, urban youth life, military, nijigen (two dimensional space), etc.

中国网络文学走出国门

在过去的十几年中，中国的网络文学发展迅速，从最初零散的自发创作交流到逐步规模化，进而成为极其具有商业价值的热门互联网产业，网络文学每年吸引的读者高达几亿人次，成为中国当代文学上的奇观。

大部分人都觉得，中国的网络文学只在国内盛行，但其实它早已走出国门，走向世界，越来越多的外国朋友被中国的网络文学所吸引。

"武侠世界（WuxiaWorld）"是目前最大的、专门从事中国网络文学翻译的网站。自2014年12月建站，在两年之内，WuxiaWorld就成了全球Alexa排名前1,500的大型网站，日均页面访问量将近400万人次。读者来自全球近百个国家和地区，其中三分之一是美国读者，其余还有来自菲律宾、印度尼西亚、加拿大和德国等国家的大批读者。

在十大外国人最爱读的网络文学作品中，玄幻、仙侠题材占了一大半，"重生""穿越""长生"等情节出现率极高，丰富的想象力和鲜明的中国元素，以及作品中所传达的积极向上的生活态度是吸引国外读者的主要原因。

Chinese Network Literature Going Abroad

In the last two decades, Chinese network literature has developed rapidly. From the initial spontaneous platform for writers to communicate, it gradually grew into a popular online industry with a large scale and great commercial value. The online literary works attract reading of hundreds of millions every year, which is a miracle for Chinese contemporary literature.

Most people think that Chinese network literature is only popular in China. Actually, it has already gone abroad and marched into the world. More and more people in overseas countries are interested in Chinese network literary works.

WuxiaWorld is the biggest professional website which works on translating Chinese network literary works. It was set up in December 2014, and only within two years it became the top 1,500 websites on Alexa ranking. The average daily page visits reached nearly 4 million, including readers from nearly a hundred countries and regions all over the world. Approximately one-third of them were Americans and the rest were mainly from the Philippine, Indonesia, Canada, and Germany.

Among the top ten foreigners' favorite network literary works, the subjects of fantasy and Chinese martial arts and warriors account for more than half. The common plots are "rebirth", "time travels", and "longevity". What attracts the foreign readers is the rich imagination, distinctive Chinese elements, and the positive attitude towards life these works try to convey.

网络文学在海外的火热，也带动了一些外国人学中文的热情，很多人感慨："我为什么没有早学中文？"还有一些人，为了能看懂中文版的小说，自学中文。一些外国人在翻译长达几百万字的作品时，中文水平得到了质的飞越。

《明朝那些事儿》

《明朝那些事儿》是一部关于明朝历史的网络连载小说，于2006年3月10日开始发表在天涯社区。《明朝那些事儿》主要讲述的是从1344年到1644年这三百年间关于明朝几代皇帝的一些故事。《明朝那些事儿》参考了大量史料，以年代和具体人物为主线，并加入了小说的笔法，语言幽默风趣。尤其是对明朝官场政治、战争、帝王心理花了很多笔墨，使得一个个原本陌生、模糊的历史人物在书中变得鲜活起来。网络连载期间，每月点击率逾百万人次，先后被翻译为日文、韩文及英文等多国语言。

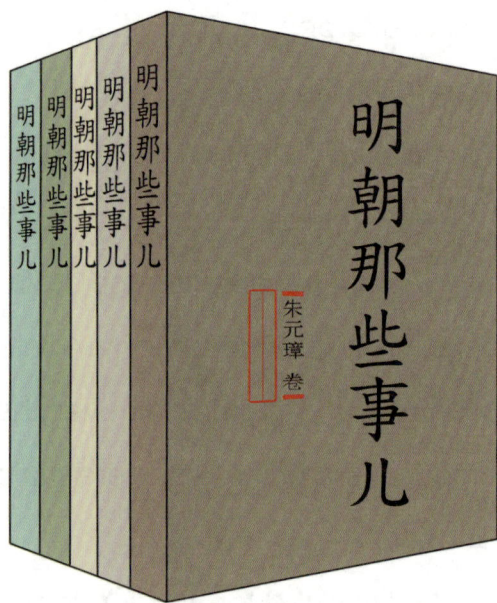

The fever of the network literature abroad has also spurred the enthusiasm of some foreigners for learning Chinese. Many of them said with regret: "Why didn't I begin to learn Chinese earlier?" In order to understand the novel in Chinese version, some even study Chinese by themselves. After translating a one-million-character literary work, they would have tremendous progress in Chinese.

Stories About the Ming Dynasty

Stories About the Ming Dynasty is an online serial novel about the Ming Dynasty, posted on the Internet forum Tianya Club since March 10, 2006. Based on a large amount of historical materials, *Stories About the Ming Dynasty* tells stories of several emperors of the Ming Dynasty between 1344 and 1644 in chronological order. Its language is humorous, with descriptions about politics, wars, and psychology of emperors in the Ming Dynasty, which makes the historical figures who were originally unfamiliar alive in the book. During the posting time, the novel achieved the monthly click-rate of over a million and was translated into many foreign languages including Japanese, Korean, English, etc.

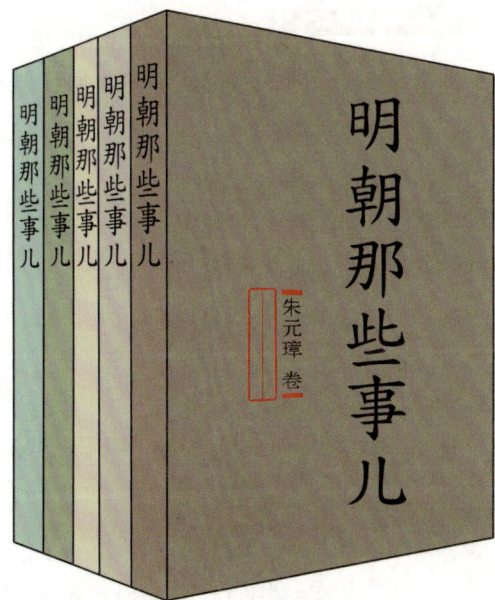

4. 重点词汇

网络文学

你觉得什么样的人喜欢看**网络文学**?

连载

现在在报纸上还有**连载**的小说吗?

玄幻 作品

你能说出一部中国的网络**玄幻作品**吗?

武侠

你知道哪些中国**武侠**电影?

二次元

"**二次元**"这个词是从哪里来的?是什么意思?

5. 实践活动

(1)请和同学讨论一下,一部成功的网络小说,需要哪些因素?

(2)请上网查找一部受欢迎的网络文学作品,并向同学做一个介绍和评论。

(3)看看那些已经被改编成影视的网络文学作品,它们有哪些共同点?

4. Keywords

network literature

What kind of people do you think is keen to read **network literature**?

serialize

Are there any novels **serialized** in newspapers now?

fantasy   literary work

Could you name one Chinese **fantasy** network **literary work**?

martial arts and warrior

Do you know films about Chinese **martial arts and warriors**?

nijigen (two dimensional space)

Where was the word "**nijigen**" originated? What does it mean?

5. Activities

(1) Discuss with your classmates what contributes to the success of a network novel.

(2) Surf the Internet for a popular network literary work, introduce it to your classmates and make your own comments.

(3) Read some network literary works which have been adapted to films and TV dramas and figure out their common features.

（4）尝试和同学一起表演网络文学的某个片段。

（5）如果你想写网络小说，你会写什么类型的？为什么？

6. 自我评估

	😊	😐	😞
（1）我能说出一些影响广泛的中国网络文学作品的名字。			
（2）我能说明中国网络文学的发展情况。			
（3）我能说明影响中国网络文学发展的因素。			

(4) Try to role play one part of a story in a network literary work with your classmates.

(5) If you were to write a network novel, what type of work would you create? Why?

6. Self-assessment

	☺	😐	☹
(1) I can name some influential Chinese network literary works.			
(2) I can tell the development of Chinese network literature.			
(3) I can tell the factors making an impact on the development of Chinese network literature.			

第九课　中国功夫

1. 学习目标

（1）能说明武术和功夫的异同。

（2）能说明外家拳和内家拳的区别。

（3）能说明少林寺功夫的主要特点。

（4）能说明功夫与跆拳道、泰拳的异同。

2. 热身活动

讨论

（1）你看过功夫电影吗？你最喜欢的功夫明星有哪些？

（2）你听说过少林寺吗？

（3）你觉得功夫和空手道、拳击等有什么异同？

（4）你看过中国古代的武器吗？你知道它们的名称吗？

Lesson Nine   Chinese Kung Fu

1. Learning objectives

(1) Be able to tell the differences between martial arts and Kung Fu.

(2) Be able to illustrate the differences between *Waijiaquan* (External Boxing Arts) and *Neijiaquan* (Internal Boxing Arts).

(3) Be able to introduce the main characteristics of Shaolin Kung Fu.

(4) Be able to illustrate the similarities and differences among Kung Fu, taekwondo, and Thai boxing.

2. Warm-up

Discussion

(1) Have you ever seen Kung Fu films? Who are your favorite Kung Fu stars?

(2) Have you ever heard of the Shaolin Temple?

(3) What are the similarities and differences among Kung Fu, karate, and boxing?

(4) Have you ever seen some ancient Chinese weapons? Do you know their names?

3. 阅读课文

武术和功夫

　　中国武术是中国传统文化的重要一环。中国武术往往带有思想冶炼的文化特征及人文哲学的特色、意义，对现今中国的大众文化有着深远影响。

　　中国武术的起源可以追溯到原始社会。当时，人类用棍棒等工具与野兽搏斗，逐渐积累了一些攻防经验，后来慢慢发展成强身健体的技术。据传华佗首创"五禽戏"，是中国武术的滥觞。

3. Reading texts

Martial Arts and Kung Fu

Chinese martial arts are an important part of Chinese traditional culture. Incorporating the essences of Chinese culture, ideology, and philosophy, they have a profound influence on the mass culture of today's China.

The origin of Chinese martial arts can be traced back to the primitive society, when humans combated with beasts using tools such as sticks and gradually accumulated some experience in fight and defense, which later developed into arts of strengthening bodies. It is said that "Wu Qin Xi" (The Five Animal Frolics), which was first created by Hua Tuo, is the beginning of Chinese martial arts.

　　由于历史发展和地域分布关系，中国武术衍生出了不同的流派。据统计，中国目前有"历史清楚，脉络有序，风格独特，自成体系"的拳种约300多种。改革开放后，一般按其内容分为套路和搏击格斗两个类别。目前中国武术主要包括搏击技巧、格斗手法、攻防策略和武器使用等技术。

　　武术在历史上有很多称呼，古称相搏、手搏、卞、弁、白打、武功、国术或武艺等，1949年国家体育运动委员会将其正式更名为"武术"，强调是以中华文化为理论基础，以技击方法为基本内容，以套路、格斗、功法为主要运动形式的传统体育。

　　功夫一般是国外人对武术的称呼，也是广东地区人们对武术的称呼，更多是指南拳类拳术。"功夫"一词在两百年前就被到中国来的法国传教士传到欧洲，但是它未普及于欧美。直到20世纪60年代，随着李小龙的功夫片播放，"功夫"才逐渐被传播开。

Numerous schools of Chinese martial arts have come into being as a result of historical development and geographical distribution. It is calculated that up to now there are over 300 types of *Quan* (boxing) in China, which have clear historical records, orderly development, unique styles, and self-consistent systems. After China's implementation of reform and opening-up policy, according to their contents, Chinese martial arts are generally classified into two categories, *Taolu* (an exhibition and full-contact sport of bare-hand and weapon forms) and boxing or fighting technique. Chinese martial arts now include boxing, fighting technique, combat and defense tactics, weapon practice, etc.

Chinese martial arts had various names in history. It was called xiāngbó (相搏), shǒubó (手搏), biàn (卞), biàn (弁), báidǎ (白打), wǔgōng (武功), guóshù (国术), or wǔyì (武艺) in ancient times. In 1949 the State Sports Commission officially changed its name into "Wushu" (martial arts) emphasizing that based on the Chinese culture, Chinese martial arts were a traditional sport about fighting skills and techniques in forms of *Taolu*, wrestling, and laws for *Gong*.

Kung Fu is a term commonly used by foreigners and Cantonese for Wushu. Nevertheless, more often it refers to the boxing techniques of *Nan Quan* (Nan Boxing). The word "Kung Fu" was brought to Europe by French missionaries who came to China two hundred years ago, but it was not popularized in Europe and America until 1960s when Bruce Lee's Kung Fu movies were put on show.

外家拳和内家拳

中国拳法分成内家拳和外家拳，外家拳以练力为主，讲究外型，如少林、洪拳、螳螂、截拳道等。内家拳以练气为主，讲究内修，如太极、形意、八卦、大成等。

外家拳是利用局部暴发的力量打击对手；内家拳是用整体力打人，其特征是局部肌肉用力很小，便可将对手轻易击倒。外家拳强调先发制人，抢先出手，包括使用预先练熟的连环招法攻击对手。而内家拳则是后发制人，根据对手的招式和劲力来决定自己的招式和发力方法。一般而言，练外家拳的拳手大多肌肉发达，棱角分明，特别是有些拳手挺胸收腹时，八块腹肌非常凸出。但内家拳手，一般放松时胳膊上的肌肉不带棱角，同时腹部多是前凸，不易看到腹肌。

External Boxing Arts and Internal Boxing Arts

Chinese boxing arts are classified into two categories: the External Boxing Arts and the Internal Boxing Arts. The former works on the practice of physical strength and gives importance to the physical shape, such as Shaolin, Hung Gar, Mantis Boxing, and Jeet Kune Do, while the latter focuses on the practice of *qi* (breath, energy flow) giving importance to internal practice, such as Taiji, Xingyi, Baguazhang, and Dacheng quan.

In the External Boxing Arts, practitioners attack their opponents with sudden outbursts of explosive movement of a body part, while in the Internal Boxing Arts, practitioners knock down their opponents easily with the strengths of their whole body instead of using one part of their body. The External Boxing Arts emphasize the tactic of gaining the initiative by striking the first blow including attacking the opponents with sets of movements which have been skillfully practiced, while the Internal Boxing Arts emphasize the tactic of gaining dominance by striking only after the opponent has struck. The opponent's strength and movements decide one's movements and the way to generate his/her power. Generally speaking, the practitioners of the External Boxing Arts look muscular, especially when they square their shoulders and tighten their abdominal muscles. In contrast, when the practitioners of the Internal Boxing Arts are relaxed, their muscles in the arms do not stand out and their bellies look bulging, but their muscles are not apparent.

尽管外家拳和内家拳有很多区别，但是其实两者又有关联。外家拳以刚猛为主，刚中有柔；内家拳以柔为主，积柔成刚。中国武术界强调"内外兼练"。

太　极　拳

太极拳是以中国传统儒、道哲学中的太极、阴阳辩证理念为核心思想，集颐养性情、强身健体、技击对抗等多种功能为一体的中国传统拳术。目前太极拳分成比武用的太极拳、体操运动用的太极操和太极推手等几种形式。

传统太极拳门派众多，常见的太极拳流派有陈式、杨式、武式、吴式、孙式、和式等派别，各派既有传承关系，各有自己的特点，也相互借鉴，呈百花齐放之态。由于太极拳是近代形成的拳种，流派众多，群众基础广泛，因此是中国武术拳种中非常具有生命力的一支。

2006年，太极拳被列为首批国家级非物质文化遗产。

Although the External and Internal Boxing Arts differ a lot with each other, they are actually closely related. The External Boxing Arts give much importance to hardness and ferocity, which is coupled with softness, while the Internal Boxing Arts give much importance to softness, which is gathered and transferred into hardness. Therefore, practitioners are encouraged to practice both external and internal arts in the circle of Chinese Martial Arts.

Taiji (Tàijíquán)

Based on the philosophy of keeping balance between the forces of *yin* and *yang* in traditional Chinese Confucianism and Daoism, Taiji is a type of *Quan* (fist) in the traditional Chinese Martial Arts practiced for its function in disposition development, health benefit and defense training. Taiji is now practiced for martial competitions, which is called Taijiquan (Taiji Fist) , and for athletic sports such as Taiji exercise, *tui shou* (pushing hands), etc.

The traditional Taiji is abundant in schools, among which there are some popular ones such as Chen Style, Yang Style, Wu (wǔ) Style, Wu (wú) Style, Sun Style, and He Style. Having their own unique characteristics, these schools are closely related. At the same time, they learn from each other, which contributes to the free development of different styles like all flowers in blossom. As a modern type of *Quan*, Taiji has become a vital Chinese martial art thanks to its various schools and a large number of practitioners.

In 2006, Taiji was put on the first list of national intangible cultural heritage.

少 林 寺

　　少林寺位于河南省登封市嵩山五乳峰下，坐落于嵩山腹地少室山茂密的树林中，"少林寺"之名由此而来。少林寺始建于北魏太和十九年，是我国久负盛名的佛教寺院。历代少林武僧潜心研创少林功夫，让少林寺成了功夫的发祥地，所以有"天下功夫出少林，少林功夫甲天下"之说。少林功夫历代传习的功夫套数有数百种，还有擒拿、格斗、点穴、气功等多种门类独特的功法。在唐代，由于朝廷的大力支持，少林寺发展得非常快，得到"天下第一名刹"的美称，少林功夫也从此变得家喻户晓。民国时期，军阀石友三放火烧毁了寺里的大部分建筑，少林寺几乎毁于一旦。

　　中华人民共和国成立后，少林寺在国家的支持下重振当年的雄风，特别是1982年一部《少林寺》电影，使少林寺、少林功夫名扬天下。少林寺自建成以

The Shaolin Temple

The Shaolin Temple is located at the foot of Wurufeng of Song Mountain, Dengfeng City, Henan Province. The Shaolin Temple got its name because it stands among the dense forests of Shaoshi Mountain in the hinterland of Song Mountain. Set up in the 19th year of Taihe in the Northern Wei Dynasty (495 A.D.), the Shaolin Temple has had a reputation as a top buddhist temple in China for a long time. It is the cradle for Shaolin Kung Fu, where the martial monks through the ages have dedicated themselves to the practice and creation of Shaolin Kung Fu. Hence, there is a saying that "The world's best Kung Fu is born in Shaolin and Shaolin Kung Fu is the best in the world". There are as many as several hundred series of Shaolin Kung Fu skills handed down and practiced over generations. In addition, there are all kinds of special bodies of Kung Fu techniques such as grappling, wrestling, attacking a vital point of the body, and Qigong. In the Tang Dynasty, with the support of the imperial court, the Shaolin Temple grew so rapidly that it won a good reputation as the World's First Temple and Shaolin Kung Fu became a household name. However, during 1912–1949, the warlord Shi Yousan set fire to the Shaolin Temple, which burnt most of the buildings in the temple and the Shaolin Temple was nearly destroyed.

After the establishment of the People's Republic of China, with the support of the State, the Shaolin Temple revived the glory of its old time. Especially when the movie *The Shaolin Temple* was put on show in 1982, both the Shaolin Temple and Shaolin Kung Fu became world-renowned. Since its establishment, the Shaolin

来，积淀了丰厚的历史内涵和文化底蕴，每年接待游客150余万人次，成为中国的旅游胜地。

十八般兵器

中国古典武侠小说中经常说"十八般武艺样样精通"，主要是形容精通各种武艺的人。这样的人往往具备使用十八般兵器的技能和功夫。十八般兵器根据年代和地区的不同，其内容也有所不同。

如今的武术界普遍认为十八般兵器是指刀、枪、剑、戟、斧、钺、钩、叉、鞭、锏、锤、抓、镗、棍、槊、棒、拐、流星。

Temple has accumulated rich historical connotations and cultural heritage. As a famous tourist attraction, it receives more than 1.5 million visits every year.

Eighteen Arms

In Chinese martial arts fictions, some figures are often depicted as masters of eighteen martial arts, which implies that they are good at all types of martial arts and proficient in using the eighteen arms. But the exact list of the eighteen arms varies from different times and regions.

However, the list which is popular in today's Chinese Martial Arts circle contains the following weapons: *dāo* (sabre), *qiāng* (spear), *jiàn* (straight sword), *jǐ* (halberd), *fǔ* (axe), *yuè* (battle axe), *gōu* (hook sword), *chā* (fork), *biān* (chain whip), *jiǎn* (mace), *chuí* (hammer), *zhuā* (talon), *táng* (trident-halberd), *gùn*(cudgel), *shuò* (a long spear), *bàng* (short cudgel), *guǎi* (crutch), and *liúxīng* (meteor hammer).

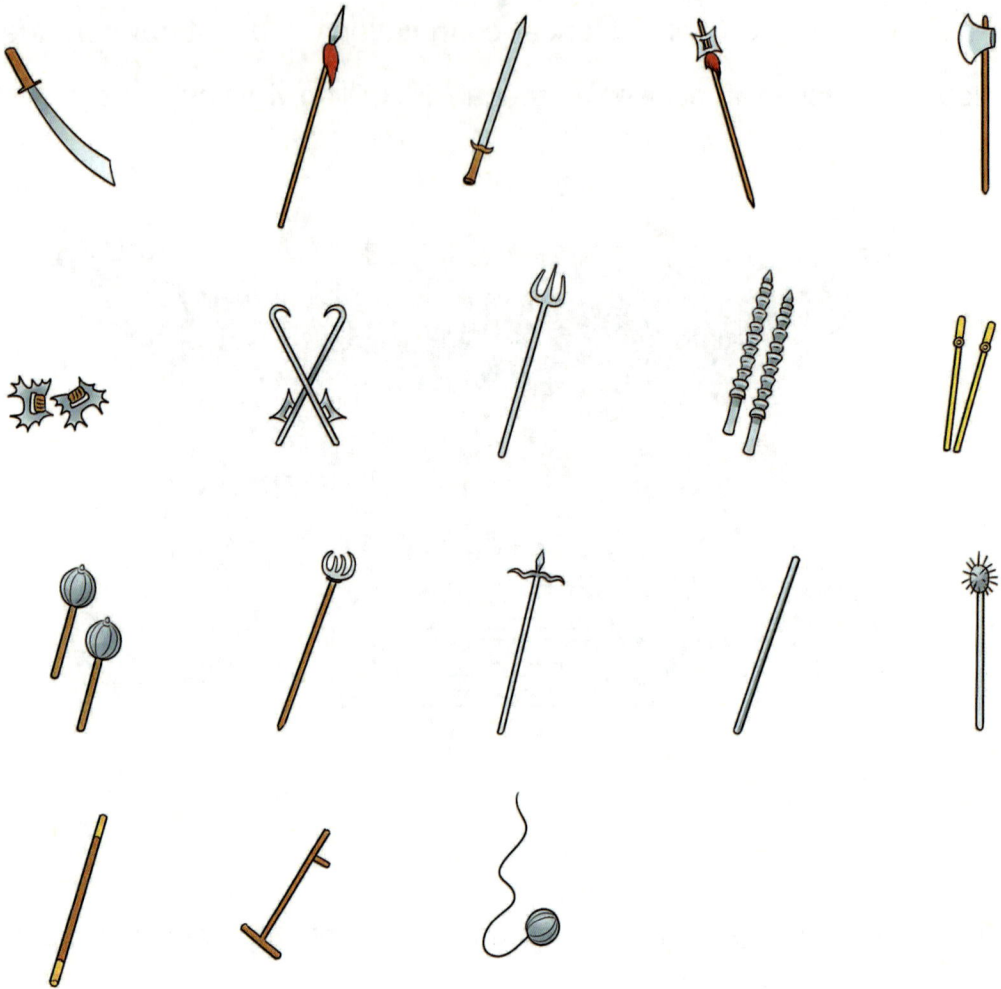

4. 重点词汇

武术

你想练习**武术**吗？

功夫

你知道哪些中国**功夫**电影明星？

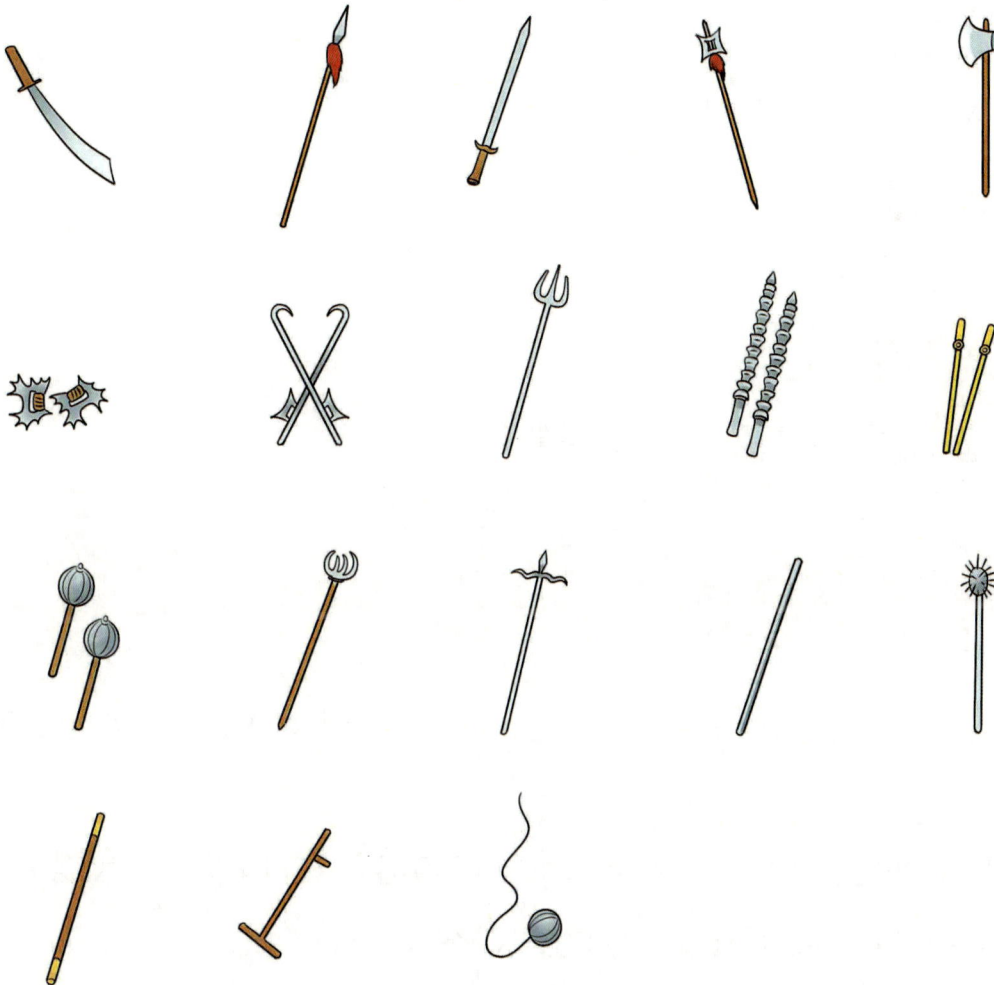

4. Keywords

martial arts

Do you want to practice **martial arts**?

Kung Fu

What Chinese **Kung Fu** stars do you know?

太极拳

打**太极拳**有什么好处?

少林寺

少林寺在哪里?

兵器

你在电影中常常看见哪些中国**兵器**?

5. 实践活动

（1）去清晨的公园里看看，哪些人在练习中国功夫？他们练习的是什么功夫？

（2）李小龙、李连杰、成龙等功夫电影明星，在其电影中所表现出来的功夫特点各有不同，请分析比较他们功夫风格的异同。

（3）查找资料，向同学介绍自己感兴趣的某种中国功夫。

（4）中国功夫与跆拳道、空手道和泰拳的区别是什么？请选择你熟悉的一种进行比较。

（5）中国功夫在现代是否还有存在的价值和意义？你认为为什么很多人会喜欢练习中国功夫？

Taijiquan

What are the benefits of practicing **Taijiquan**?

the Shaolin Temple

Where is **the Shaolin Temple** located?

weapon

What Chinese **weapons** do you often see in the movies?

5. Activities

(1) Go to a park in the morning and observe who is practicing Chinese Kung Fu. What type of Kung Fu are they practicing?

(2) Known as popular Chinese Kung Fu movie stars, Bruce Lee, Jet Li, and Jackie Chen perform Kung Fu of their own styles in the movies. Analyze and compare the similarities and differences among these styles.

(3) Search for information and introduce to your classmates a type of Chinese Kung Fu that you are most interested in.

(4) What are the differences among Chinese Kung Fu, taekwondo, karate, and Thai boxing? You can compare Chinese Kung Fu with one of the other three that you know the best.

(5) What is the value and significance of Chinese Kung Fu in the modern times? Why do many people love practicing Chinese Kung Fu?

6. 自我评估

	😊	😐	😞
（1）我能说明武术和功夫的异同。			
（2）我能说明内家拳和外家拳的区别。			
（3）我能说明少林寺功夫的主要特点。			
（4）我能说明功夫与跆拳道、泰拳的异同。			

6. Self-assessment

	🙂	😐	🙁
(1) I can tell the similarities and differences between martial arts and Kung Fu.			
(2) I can differ the Internal Boxing Arts from the External Boxing Arts.			
(3) I can introduce the main characteristics of Shaolin Kung Fu.			
(4) I can tell the similarities and differences among Kung Fu, taekwondo and Thai boxing.			

第十课　中国教育

1. 学习目标

（1）能说明中国基础教育的基本情况。

（2）能说明中国教育中的常见名词，如中考、高考等。

（3）能比较中外的教育制度。

2. 热身活动

讨论

（1）在你们国家，小学到初中有没有升学考试？初中到高中呢？

（2）如果不上高中，初中毕业后学生有几种选择？

（3）在你们国家，几岁可以上学？小学、初中、高中分别要读几年？中国呢？

（4）你们国家有没有私立学校？它们和公立学校有什么异同？中国有没有私立学校？

Lesson Ten   Education in China

1. Learning Objectives

(1) Be able to talk about elementary education in China.

(2) Be able to explain some common terms about education in China, such as *Zhongkao* (entrance examination for senior high school, or middle technical school) and *Gaokao* (The National College Entrance Examination).

(3) Be able to compare and contrast the Chinese education system with that of the foreign countries.

2. Warm-up

Discussion

(1) Is there an entrance exam from primary school to junior high school in your country? How about for entering senior high school?

(2) What are the other options for those who do not go to senior high school after they graduate from junior high school?

(3) What is the schooling age in your country? How many years do you have to study in primary school, junior high school, and senior high school respectively? How about the situation in China?

(4) Are there any private schools in your country? What are the similarities and differences between a private school and a public school? Are there any private schools in China?

（5）你在中学学习哪些科目？你最喜欢的科目和不喜欢的科目有哪些？

3. 阅读课文

学 前 教 育

中国的学前教育是针对0-6岁幼儿进行的，实施学前教育的机构主要是托儿所和幼儿园，托儿所接收0-3岁的幼儿，幼儿园接收3岁以上的幼儿。

幼儿园一般读三年，分为小班、中班、大班，日常开展以游戏为主的活动，向幼儿进行与他们年龄相适合的教学活动，促进幼儿在体育、智育、德育、美育方面的全面和谐发展，也为他们进入小学学习做好准备。

除此之外，学前教育能够为幼儿提供健康丰富的生活和活动环境，让忙于工作的家长得以放心。目前中国的学前教育按照国家、集体、公民个人一起办的原则，

(5) What subjects do you study in high school? What are your favorite subjects and the subjects that you do not like?

3. Reading texts

Preschool Education

In China, preschool education is the education for children from zero to six years old. The two educational establishments offering preschool education are nursery schools accepting infants from zero to three years old, and kindergartens accepting children over three years old.

Generally speaking, kindergartens offer three years' schooling including bottom class, middle class, and top class. Daily game-based teaching activities which suit children's ages are organized and held to promote their all-round and harmonious development of physical, intellectual, moral and aesthetics qualities and get them ready for entry into primary school.

Moreover, preschool education provides healthy and colorful environment for children where they could live and do activities so that their parents can focus on their work. At present, preschool education in China develops in multiple channels and forms in accordance with the principle of running

多渠道、多形式地发展，形成了各种各样的公立和私立的托儿所、幼儿园，学前教育在中国得到快速发展。

基 础 教 育

基础教育是造就人才的第一步，中国的基础教育包括义务教育和高中教育。

义务教育由国家免费提供，所有的适龄儿童、少年都必须接受。2000年，中国基本普及了义务教育，扫除了青壮年的文盲现象。2005年开始，义务教育阶段的入学率稳定在99%以上，九年义务教育的政策得到彻底的贯彻执行。当学生处于义务教育阶段时，学校不能以任何理由劝退、开除学生，如果学生多次违反校纪校规，学校可以采取批评、记错等方式进行处分。

义务教育包括小学和初中两个阶段共九年的时间。义务教育阶段的学习科目主要有：语文、英语、数学、物理、化学、生物、政治、地理、历史以及音乐、体育、美术等，所有科目的教学目标及内容均由国家相关教育部门制定课程标准。从小学进入初中学习不需要进行升学考试，所有完成了小学课程的学

schools together with the State, the collective, and the individual citizens. As a result, various public and private nurseries and kindergartens have been established and preschool education in China is developing rapidly.

Elementary Education

Elementary education is the first step to cultivate a person's ability, which includes compulsory education and high school education in China.

Compulsory education is funded by the State, which all children and juveniles of school age must receive. In 2000, China popularized compulsory education and eliminated the illiteracy of young adults. Since 2005, the enrollment rate of children of compulsory education age has stabilized at more than 99%, which signifies that the policy of nine-year compulsory education has been carried out completely. During the compulsory education period, the schools are not allowed to persuade any students to quit school or expel them for any reason. However, if a student repeatedly violates the school discipline and regulations, the school could take disciplinary action by means of criticizing and recording a demerit.

Compulsory education includes all together nine years of primary school and junior high school. The subjects covered in the compulsory education period are mainly listed as follows: Chinese, English, Mathematics, Physics, Chemistry, Biology, Politics, Geography, History, Music, P.E., the Fine Arts, etc. The criteria for all the curricula including teaching objectives and contents of these subjects are drafted by the national education departments. No entrance examination is required from primary school to junior high school. After graduating from the

生都可以进入初中学习。

　　九年义务教育是促进教育公平的重要方式，对提高国民素质有重要意义。学生在完成义务教育之后，即初中学习阶段结束，通过考试，成绩合格，就可以进入高中阶段的教育。这个阶段的教育大致可以分为两类，一类是普通高中，其毕业生通过参加国家组织的高考，进入大学继续学习；另一类是职业教育，学生具体学习在就业中所需的技能和素质，把自己培养成技术工人。

高　等　教　育

　　高等教育是为了培养高级社会人才进行的专门教育，目前中国有近三千所普通高等学校，在校本科、专科学生达三千多万人，是世界高等教育最庞大的

primary school, graduates can directly enter into junior high school.

Nine-year compulsory education is an important way to promote education equity, meanwhile, it is of great significance to improving the quality of the people of a nation. After completing the compulsory education at the end of the junior high school period, students are supposed to take certain tests. If they pass the tests, they could enter the senior high school period, which is classified into two categories: regular senior high school whose graduates will take the college entrance exam to study further at college, and vocational high school where students learn specific occupational skills and qualify them to be skilled workers.

Higher Education

Higher education is a specialized education cultivating high-level personnel for the society. At present, there are nearly 3,000 regular higher education institutions in China and the total number of the undergraduates and students at professional colleges has reached more than 30 million, which is considered

国家之一。中国的高等教育包括专科教育、本科教育和研究生教育。

专科是大学的学历层次之一，承担专科教育的机构主要是高职、高专以及部分大学。专科学校培养技术性人才，学习时间一般是2-3年，毕业时发放毕业证书。

大学本科教育是高等教育的基本组成部分。进入大学本科教育的方式主要有以下几种：一是参加高考，二是参加高校的自主招生考试，三是通过保送进入大学学习，四是专科学生通过考试从专科学校升入本科学校。上述几种途径进入的都是全日制本科，除此之外，中国还有非全日制本科，主要分为自考本科、成人高考、远程教育、业余教育、开放教育等多种类型，没有固定修业年限，学习方式多种多样，学生既可以在相关教育机构学习，也可以自学。

研究生教育分为硕士和博士两个层次，其培养或在普通高等院校，或在科研院所进行。硕士研究生的学习时间一般为2-3年，博士研究生为3-4年。博士

one of the largest higher education system in the world. Higher education in China includes professional college education, undergraduate education, and postgraduate education.

Academically, professional college education offers the professional college education degree by higher vocational colleges, junior colleges and certain universities. A professional college cultivates technical talents. A diploma will be issued upon graduation after a student spends two or three years studying there.

Undergraduate education is an essential part of higher education. There are mainly four ways to have an access to undergraduate education: Firstly, take college entrance examination; secondly, take tests organized independently by colleges and universities; thirdly, be recommended to universities and colleges without taking the entrance examination; fourthly, students at professional colleges enter colleges and universities by taking required tests. Students admitted through any of the above-mentioned ways are full-time undergraduate students. In addition, students can also study part-time in various ways including undergraduate courses for those taking "self-taught" examination and taking college entrance examination for self-taught adults, distance education, spare time education, and open education, to name a few major ones. Students do not have fixed years of study and can study in many ways. They can either study in the relevant educational institutions or learn by themselves.

Postgraduate education involves both master's programs and doctoral programs, which are completed either in the regular higher education institutions or research institutes. Generally speaking, a master's degree could be obtained

是中国最高的学位。

现在有越来越多的外国学生来中国留学，在中国的高等院校里攻读不同专业的学士、硕士和博士学位。

中考和高考

中考是初中学业水平考试的简称。它是检测初中在校生是否达到初中学业水平的水平性考试，是初中毕业证发放的必要条件。同时，中考成绩也是高中选拔学生的依据。学生可根据中考成绩报考相应的高中、中专、技校等。

高考是普通高等学校招生全国统一考试的简称。高考由教育部统一组织调度，由教育部考试中心或实行自主命题的省市级教育考试院命制试题。2001年，教育部放宽了报名参加普通高等学校招生全国统一考试的考生条件，取消了普通高考报名年龄不超过25岁、未婚的限制，中等职业学校毕业生也不再只限报

after two or three years of study while a doctoral degree could be obtained after three or four years of study. The Ph.D. is the highest academic degree in China.

More and more foreign students are coming to study in China pursuing bachelor's degree, master's degree and doctoral degree in different majors in Chinese higher education institutions.

Zhongkao (Entrance Examination for Senior High School, or Middle Technical School) and *Gaokao* (The National College Entrance Examination)

Zhongkao is an abbreviation for the Academic Examination for Junior High School Students, which checks whether students have reached the academic level for the junior high school. Students must take this test before they are issued the graduation certificate. Meanwhile, senior high schools select their students in enrollment according to the scores the students achieve in *Zhongkao*. Students apply for either regular senior high schools, secondary skill schools or technical high schools based on their results of *Zhongkao*.

Gaokao is an abbreviation for the National College Entrance Examination. It is organized and managed by the Ministry of Education and the test papers are either proposed and made by the Test Center of the Ministry of Education or the institutes of educational testing service of provinces or municipalities who are supposed to make the test papers by themselves. In 2001, the Ministry of Education loosened registration requirements for the National College Entrance Examination by removing the restriction that the candidates must be under 25 and unmarried. The graduates of secondary vocational schools are no longer

高等职业学校，也可报考普通高校。报名并参加普通高考将不受年龄及婚否的限制与影响。

4. 重点词汇

基础教育

中国的**基础教育**指的是什么？

义务教育

在中国，**义务教育**有几年？

职业教育

职业教育对中国的发展有什么好处？

课程标准

在你们国家，有没有国家制定的统一的**课程标准**？

高等教育

在你们国家，**高等教育**一般学习几年？

中考

你们国家有没有**中考**？

高考

你们国家有没有**高考**？

restricted to enter higher vocational schools, but can also apply for colleges and universities. Therefore, registration and participation in the National College Entrance Examination will not be restricted or affected by age and marital status.

4. Keywords

elementary education

What does **elementary education** in China refer to?

compulsory education

How many years does **compulsory education** last in China?

vocational education

What benefits does the **vocational education** bring to the development of China?

curriculum criteria

Is there a set of unified national **curriculum criteria** in your country?

higher education

How many years do students in your country have to study during **higher education**?

***Zhongkao* (Entrance Examination for Senior High School, or Middle Technical School)**

Is there *Zhongkao* in your country?

***Gaokao* (The National College Entrance Examination)**

Is there *Gaokao* in your country?

5. 实践活动

（1）根据"中国教育体系流程图"，向同学介绍一下中国的教育体系。

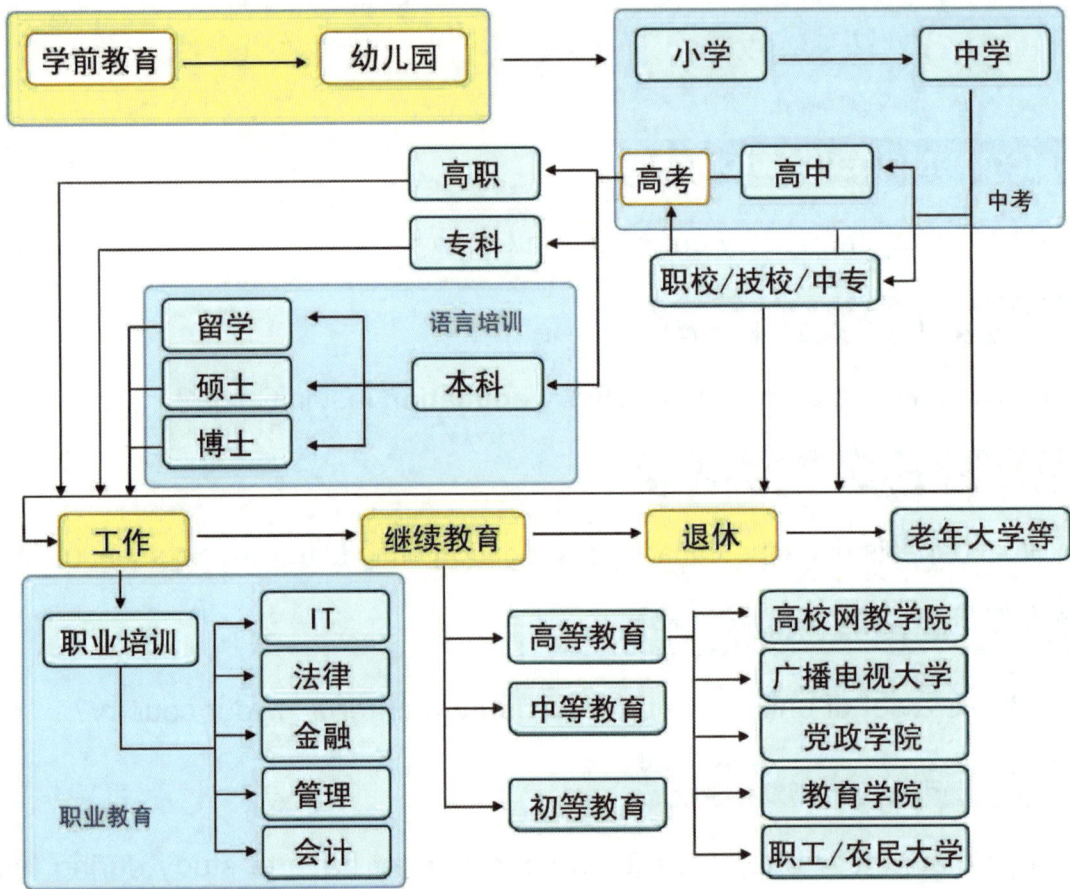

中国教育体系流程图

（2）义务教育指的是什么？为什么国家要开展义务教育？

5. Activities

(1) Look at the "Flow Chart of the Educational System in China" and introduce the educational system in China to your classmates.

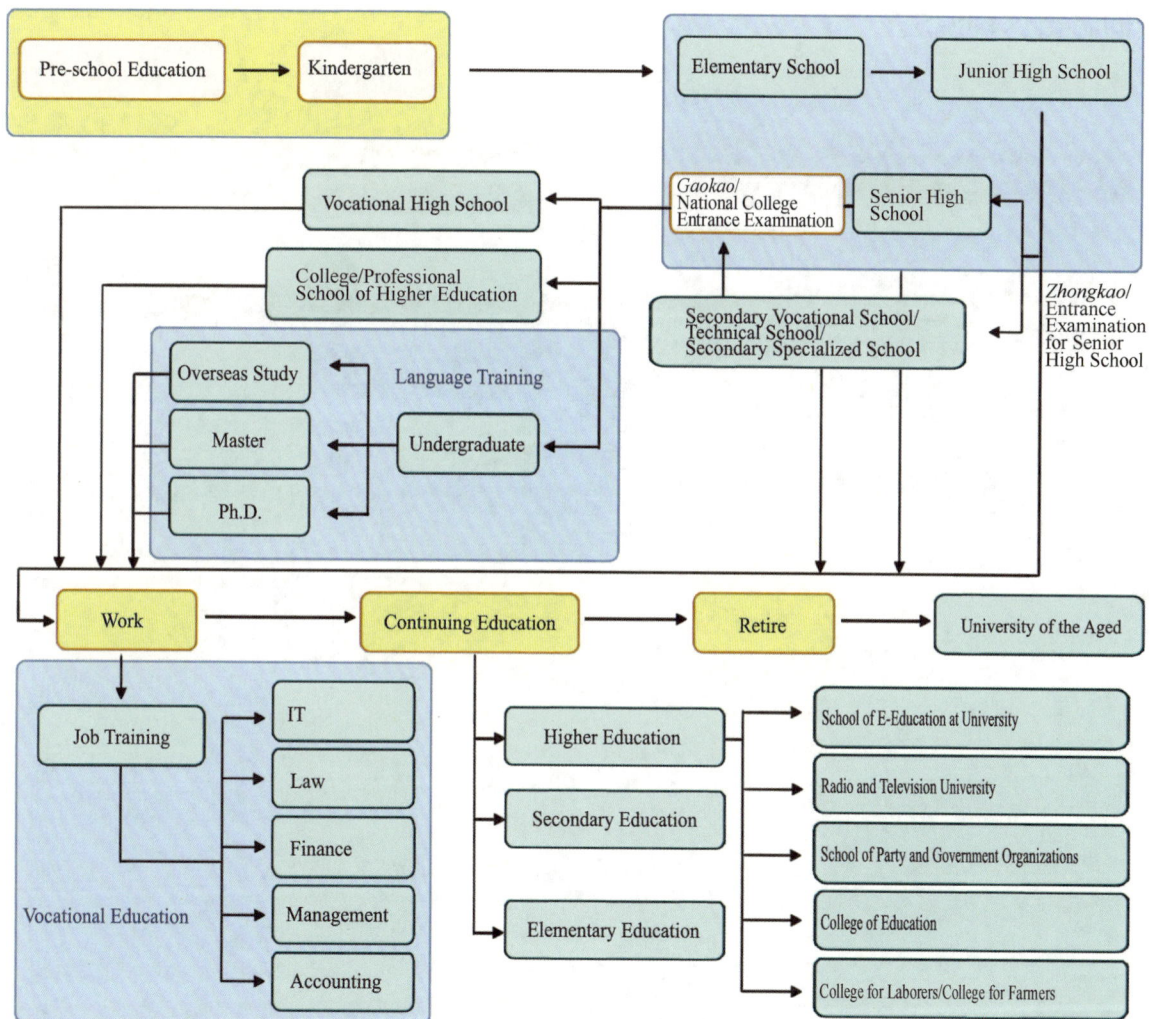

| Pre-school Education | → | Kindergarten |

Flow Chart of the Educational System in China

(2) What is compulsory education? Why is compulsory education carried out in some countries?

（3）上网查阅资料，研究一下目前中国的外来人口能否在本地上学。

（4）比较中国的教育体系和你们国家的异同，并与同学交流一下。

（5）很多中国学生会在课外参加辅导班，你们国家有类似的情况吗？

（6）中国目前是九年义务教育，有人提出应该建立十二年的义务教育。你如何看待这种说法？

6. 自我评估

	😊	😐	😞
（1）我能说明中国基础教育的基本情况。			
（2）我能说明中国教育中的常见名词，如中考、高考等。			
（3）我能比较中外的教育制度。			

(3) Surf the Internet and find out whether migrants in China are now eligible to study at local schools.

(4) Compare Chinese educational system with the one in your country and exchange your ideas with your classmates.

(5) Many Chinese students take extra tutoring classes after class. Is there a similar phenomeon in your country?

(6) Nowadays, China has nine years of compulsory education. However, some people propose twelve years of compulsory education. What's your opinion on this?

6. Self-assessment

	😊	😐	☹️
(1) I can tell the basic situation of Chinese elementary education.			
(2) I can illustrate some common terms about Chinese education such as *Zhongkao* and *Gaokao*.			
(3) I can compare the Chinese educational system with those of foreign countries.			

第十一课　太空科技

1. 学习目标

（1）能说明人造卫星的作用。

（2）能说明全球卫星定位系统及其作用。

（3）能说明中国在探索月球方面的成就。

（4）能讲述嫦娥奔月的故事。

2. 热身活动

讨论

（1）卫星、行星、恒星有什么不同？

（2）哪个国家发射了世界上第一颗人造卫星？为什么要发射人造卫星？

（3）中国什么时候发射了第一颗人造卫星？中国的人造卫星叫什么名字？

（4）GPS用中文怎么说？GPS有什么用？你知道"北斗"吗？

3. 阅读课文

人 造 卫 星

　　人造卫星是环绕着地球运行的无人航天器，科学家需要用火箭或者其他运载工具把它发射到事先设定的轨道上，以便进行探测或科学研究。人造卫星一

Lesson Eleven　Space Science & Technology

1. Learning objectives

(1) Be able to illustrate the functions of man-made satellites.

(2) Be able to describe GPS and its functions.

(3) Be able to introduce the achievements China has made in exploring the moon.

(4) Be able to tell the story of "Chang'e Flying to the Moon".

2. Warm-up

Discussion

(1) What are the differences among satellites, planets, and stars?

(2) Which country launched the first man-made satellite in the world? Why was the satellite launched?

(3) When did China launch its first man-made satellite? What was its name?

(4) What is the Chinese expression for GPS? What are the functions of GPS? Do you know "BeiDou" (BeiDou Navigation Satellite System)?

3. Reading texts

Man-Made Satellites

A man-made satellite is an unmanned spacecraft that orbits the earth, which scientists launch with rockets or by other means of transport into a pre-defined

共分为科学卫星、技术试验卫星和应用卫星三大类。1957年10月4日，苏联发射了世界上第一颗人造卫星。中国于1970年4月24日发射了第一颗人造卫星"东方红一号"，成为继美、苏、法、日等国家之后第五个制造和发射人造卫星的国家。截至2017年，中国有192颗在轨卫星，占地球卫星总数的13%，数量位居全世界第二。

全球卫星定位系统

全球卫星定位系统最初用于军事，后来转为民用，简称为GPS。GPS的运用使人类的交通变得更安全、更高效。对于大海中航行的船只或天空中飞行的

orbit for exploration or scientific research. Man-made satellites are classified into three categories: satellites for scientific purposes, technological experiment satellites, and satellites for application. On October 4, 1957, the Soviet Union launched the world's first man-made satellite. On April 24, 1970, when China launched its first man-made satellite named "Dongfanghong-1", it became the fifth country managing to manufacture and launch man-made satellites after the United States, the Soviet Union, France, and Japan. By 2017, 192 Chinese satellites were in orbit, accounting for 13% of the total number of satellites, which ranks the second in the world.

GPS (Global Positioning System)

The Global Positioning System, or GPS for short, was originally used for military purposes and later converted to civilian use. The application of GPS makes our transport safer and more efficient. In addition, with GPS ships and

飞机来说，有了全球卫星定位系统，它们不会迷失方向，并且能按最短的路线航行，从而降低运输成本。

随着科学技术的发达，GPS的接收器越来越小并开始安装在汽车上。车载GPS不仅拥有地图和定位的功能，还能告知车主到达目的地的最近路线，甚至如何避开拥堵路线。

如今，全球卫星定位系统这项技术也运用于手机导航，开发了一系列手机应用程序。比如，高德地图、百度地图和Google地图是目前中国人最喜欢的地图导航应用软件。共享单车、微信或支付宝打车等，都运用了此项技术。所以说，GPS的应用不仅提高了社会的信息化水平，也推动了数字经济的发展。

中国也开发了自己的卫星导航系统"北斗"，2011年起开始试运行。与GPS相比，北斗卫星导航系统有自己的特色——"短信服务"。一般的导航系统只是告诉你什么时间、在什么地方，而北斗卫星导航系统除此之外，还可以将你的位置发送出去，使你想告知的人获悉你的情况。

嫦娥卫星和玉兔号

探月工程是中国继人造地球卫星和载人航天之后的第三个里程碑。2004年，中国正式开展月球探测工程，命名为"嫦娥工程"。

aircraft will no longer lose direction and they can find the shortest route, thus reducing transportation costs.

With the development of science and technology, the receiver of GPS is getting smaller and smaller, enabling GPS to be installed in a car. The GPS in a car not only has maps and the function of positioning, but also can inform the driver of the nearest route to the destination and even how to avoid traffic jams.

Today, GPS is also applied for navigation on mobile phones, which contributes to the development of various Apps. For example, AMap, Baidu Maps, and Google Maps are Chinese people's favorite navigation software. This technology is even applied to the Apps such as Bike-sharing, WeChat, and taxi service on Alipay. Therefore, the application of GPS not only improves the information technology in society, but also promotes the development of the digital economy.

China has also developed its own satellite navigation system named "BeiDou", which was put into trial operation in 2011. Compared with GPS, BeiDou has its own unique characteristic, that is, message service. Generally speaking, a navigation system only tells you where you are at a certain time. But BeiDou could also send your location to the person you want to contact so he/she is well informed of your situation.

Chang'e Project and the Lunar Rover Yutu (Jade Rabbit)

The moon exploration project is the third milestone after China's man-made satellite and manned space flight. In 2004, China officially launched the moon exploration project, called the "Chang'e Project".

2007年10月24日18时05分，"嫦娥一号"成功发射升空。"嫦娥一号"是中国首颗绕月人造卫星，是以中国古代神话人物嫦娥命名的。自成功发射"嫦娥一号"后，中国相继发射了另外五颗以嫦娥命名的人造卫星。

"玉兔号"是"嫦娥三号"人造卫星月球车的名称。在中华民族神话传说中，嫦娥和玉兔都住在月宫中。传说中的玉兔善良、纯洁、敏捷，形象表达了我国和平利用太空的态度，所以月球车被命名为"玉兔号"。中国的探月工程为人类和平探索太空迈出了新的一步。

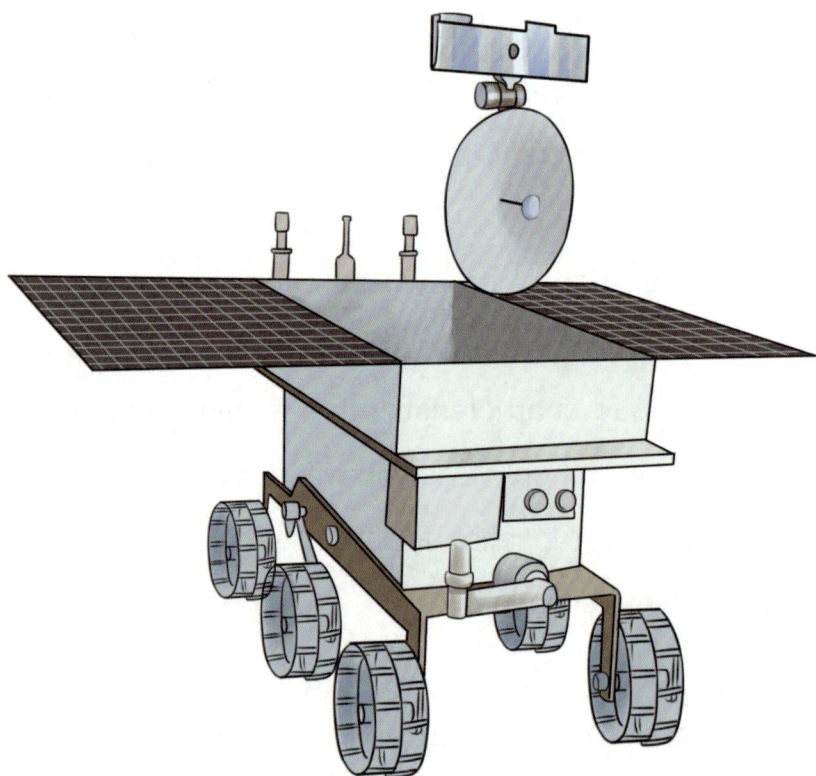

At 18:05 on October 24, 2007, "Chang'e-1" successfully launched. "Chang'e-1" is China's first man-made satellite orbiting the moon, which is named after Chang'e, a figure in ancient Chinese legends. After the successful launch of "Chang'e-1", China has launched successively another five man-made satellites named after Chang'e.

Yutu (Jade Rabbit) is the name of the lunar rover for the man-made satellite "Chang'e-3". In the Chinese fairy story, both Chang'e and the jade rabbit live on the moon. The jade rabbit is kind, pure, and agile, whose image expresses China's attitude of peaceful use of space. Therefore, the lunar rover is named Yutu. China's moon exploration project has taken a new step for human beings to explore space peacefully.

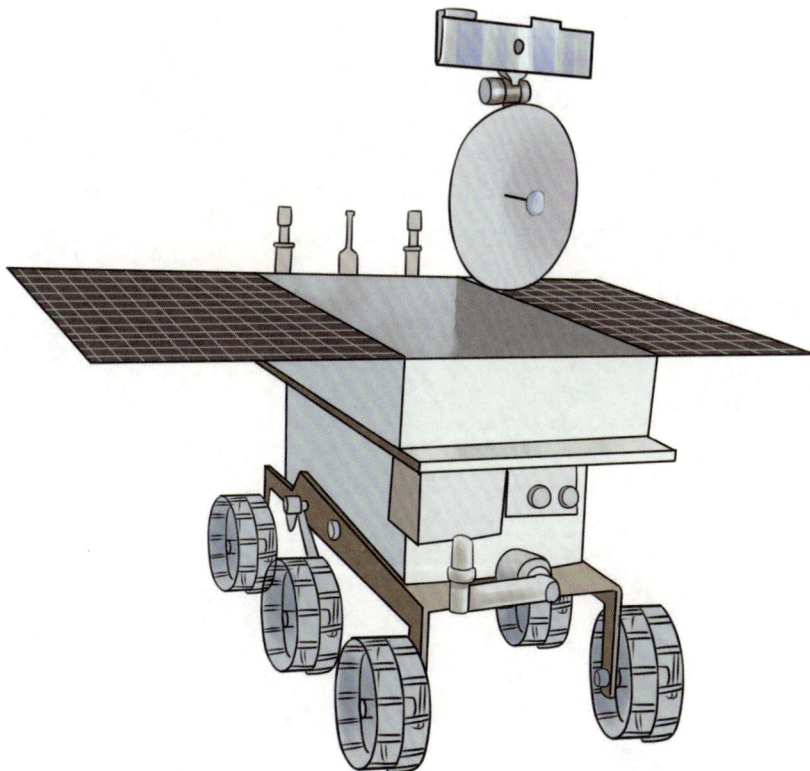

嫦娥奔月

无论是"嫦娥号"还是"玉兔号"，它们的名字都来源于中国神话故事——嫦娥奔月。

嫦娥奔月讲的是嫦娥偷吃仙丹飞向月亮的故事。据说在远古的时候，有一位射术高超的勇士叫后羿。他的妻子嫦娥又美丽又善良。有一年，天上突然出现了十个太阳，为了不让百姓遭受苦难，后羿射下九个太阳。西王母被后羿的举动所感动，送给他一颗长生不老的仙丹。奸诈的坏人一心想把仙药弄到手，于是趁后羿出门打猎后，逼迫嫦娥交出仙丹。嫦娥知道自己不是坏人的对手，危急之时她当机立断，转身打开盒子，拿出仙药吞了下去。她刚吞下仙丹，便立刻向月亮上飞去。在月亮上，不仅有桂树，还有一只玉兔，从此嫦娥便和玉兔一起守在了月宫。

Chang'e Flying to the Moon

The names of both the Chang'e Project and the lunar rover Yutu (Jade Rabbit) have their origin from the Chinese fairy tale "Chang'e Flying to the Moon".

The tale tells how Chang'e flew to the moon after she took the elixir of immortality. The legend says that there was a super archer named Houyi in the ancient times, who had a beautiful and kind wife named Chang'e. One year, ten suns rose together into the skies. To save people from the suffering, Houyi shot down nine of them. Xiwangmu (the Heavenly Empress) was moved by what Houyi had done and gave him an elixir of immortality as a reward. Then, coveting the elixir, a treacherous villain took the chance forcing Chang'e to give the elixir to him when Houyi went out hunting. Chang'e knew that she was not strong enough to fight against the villain, so that she made a quick decision in such an emergency. She turned to open the box, took out the elixir and swallowed it. As soon as she took it, she flew toward the moon and landed there. It is said that together with a cinnamon and a jade rabbit, Chang'e lives on the moon forever.

4. 重点词汇

人造卫星

中国发射的第一颗**人造卫星**叫什么？

北斗 卫星定位

北斗卫星定位有什么特点？

导航

你知道具有**导航**功能的手机软件名称吗？

嫦娥

嫦娥为什么会奔月？

5. 实践活动

（1）你们国家有没有人造卫星？人造卫星对于人们的生活有什么影响？

（2）世界上已经有GPS系统了，为什么中国还要开发北斗卫星导航系统？查阅相关资料，向同学介绍中国研发北斗卫星导航系统的背景和过程。

（3）中国的月球探测工程其实经历了非常艰苦的过程，请查找"玉兔号"的相关资料，向同学介绍一下"玉兔号"在月球上工作的情况。

4. Keywords

man-made satellite

What is the name of the first **man-made satellite** China launched?

"BeiDou" (BeiDou Navigation Satellite System) satellite positioning

What is the characteristic of **BeiDou satellite positioning**?

navigation

Can you name some **navigation** Apps for mobile phones?

Chang'e

Why did **Chang'e** fly to the moon?

5. Activities

(1) Does your country have man-made satellites? What influences does man-made satellites have on our life?

(2) Why did China develop BeiDou Satellite Navigation System even though GPS had already been invented in the world? Look up relevant information and introduce to the classmates the background and process how BeiDou Satellite Navigation System was developed.

(3) China underwent many hardships in the implementation of its moon exploration project. Look up information about the lunar rover Yutu (Jade Rabbit) and introduce to the classmates how Yutu carries out its mission on the moon.

（4）太空科技研发需要大量资金和技术，却似乎没有直接的好处。你认为一个国家有必要开展太空科技研发吗？为什么？

（5）中国人自古以来就对月亮有特殊的情感。除了嫦娥奔月，你还知道中国有哪些与月亮有关的故事、成语或者诗词？

6. 自我评估

	😊	😐	☹️
（1）我了解人造卫星的含义。			
（2）我了解全球卫星定位系统及其在导航技术中的应用。			
（3）我了解中国为探索月球作出的努力。			
（4）我会讲述嫦娥奔月的故事。			

(4) The research and development of space technology require a lot of funds and technology, but it seems that they could not bring immediate profits. Do you think that a country should develop its space technology? Why or why not?

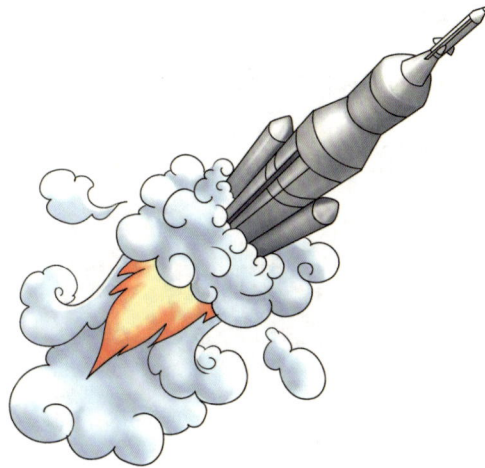

(5) Since ancient times, Chinese people have special affections for the moon. Besides "Chang'e Flying to the Moon", do you know other stories, idioms or poems related to the moon?

6. Self-assessment

	🙂	😐	☹️
(1) I know what man-made satellites are.			
(2) I know about GPS and its application to navigation.			
(3) I know the great efforts China has made to explore the moon.			
(4) I can tell the story of "Chang'e Flying to the Moon".			

第十二课 中国人的婚姻

1. 学习目标

（1）了解中西婚礼的异同。

（2）能说出中国古今婚礼的相关习俗及其流变。

（3）能说明中国家庭结构的变化。

2. 热身活动

讨论

（1）在你们国家，人们一般在哪里举行婚礼？

（2）你印象中的婚礼是什么样子的？有哪些重要的仪式？

（3）在你们国家，人们结婚时有哪些特殊的风俗？

（4）现代中国家庭结构有哪些变化？

3. 阅读课文

中国古今婚礼

提到婚礼，人们往往想到洁白的婚纱、美丽的花冠和神圣的戒指。这些纯洁的白色元素汇聚在一起，构成了大多数人对于婚礼的想象。不同于西方婚礼

Lesson Twelve   Chinese Marriages

1. Learning objectives

(1) Know the similarities and differences between Chinese and Western weddings.

(2) Be able to talk about the related customs and changes of Chinese ancient and modern weddings.

(3) Be able to talk about the changes of Chinese family structure.

2. Warm-up

Discussion

(1) Where do people usually hold wedding ceremonies in your country?

(2) What is your impression of a wedding? What are the important rituals?

(3) What are the special marriage customs in your country?

(4) What changes have taken place in the structure of modern Chinese family?

3. Reading texts

Ancient and Modern Weddings in China

When it comes to weddings, people often think of white wedding dresses, beautiful crowns, and sacred rings. These pure white elements come together to form most people's imagination of a wedding. Unlike the white wedding ceremony

的洁白，中国婚礼在中国人的心中是铺天盖地喜气洋洋的大红色。

　　在古代，中国的婚礼有着十分复杂的流程。总的来说，中国传统婚礼分为婚前礼、正婚礼、婚后礼三种。

　　在结婚之前，男女双方需要做许许多多准备工作。首先，男方需要请一位媒人代替他向中意的女方家提亲，在女方答应成亲之后，忙碌的前期工作就要开始了：男方需要准备聘书（订婚书）、礼书（礼物单）、迎书（迎亲书），同时请媒人询问女方的生辰八字，算出结婚的良辰吉日。算好日子以后，男方需要通知女方家庭，并亲自到女方家中举行订婚礼。订婚礼时，一般会送"聘金"。同样的，女方在这时也需要精心准备自己的嫁妆，并将它们尽快送往男方家，这样，两个人的婚前礼就算是正式完成了。

in the West, the Chinese wedding ceremony in the hearts of the Chinese people is the bright red.

In ancient times, Chinese weddings had a very complicated process. Generally speaking, Chinese traditional weddings can be divided into three parts: premarital ceremony, formal wedding ceremony, and postmarital ceremony.

Before getting married, both the man's family and woman's undergo many preparations. First of all, the man needs to invite a matchmaker to propose to the woman's family. After the woman promises to be married, the busy pre-work will begin: the man needs to write a betrothal letter, a gift letter and a wedding letter. At the same time, the matchmaker asks the woman's date of birth and eight characters of a horoscopedate to calculate the best day for the wedding. When the day is chosen, the man needs to inform the woman's family and go to the woman's home to hold an engagement in person. When engaged to a wedding, the "bride-price" is usually given. Similarly, a woman needs to prepare her dowry carefully and send it to her husband's home as soon as possible, so that the premarital ceremony can be officially completed.

在结婚那天，正婚礼就更加复杂。男方要亲自去女方家迎接新娘，并且要用轿子将新娘接回自己家。女方则要早早换上嫁衣，盖上绣着龙凤呈祥或者鸳鸯戏水的红盖头，等着丈夫前来迎接自己。到了夫家，就要进行婚礼中最重要的"拜堂"了。简单地说，拜堂就是男女双方行三叩之礼。他们来到夫家后，婚礼的司仪会高喊三声："一拜天地！二拜高堂！夫妻对拜！"这就是说夫妻二人要拉着结发球，先拜谢天地，再拜谢父母，最后面对面行跪拜礼。这三拜结束之后，男女双方就正式成为夫妻了。接下来就是喜宴，客人们会送上礼金（红包），祝福新人美满幸福，早生贵子。喜宴之后，夫妻二人便会进入婚房。在新房之中，中国人会点起许多红烛，夫妻二人便一起喝合卺酒，即手挽手喝交杯酒。之后，丈夫会用撑杆挑开妻子的盖头。忙碌的正婚礼到此才结束。

On the wedding day, the ceremony is more complicated. The bridegroom should go to the bride's home, and use a sedan chair to take the bride back to his home. The bride, on the other hand, needs to put on her wedding dress early and cover her head with a red veil embroidered with a dragon and a phoenix or mandarin ducks playing in the water, waiting for her husband to come to meet her. When they get to the bridegroom's home, they will have the most important ceremony. Simply put, it is the ritual of three bows of the bride and the bridegroom. The wedding master would shout three times: "The first, bow to the heaven and the earth!" "The second, bow to the parents!" "The third, bow to each other!" This means that the couple will bow, first to thank the heaven and the earth, then thank their parents, and finally thank each other face to face. Afterwards, they officially become husband and wife. Next is the wedding banquet. The guests will send gifts (red envelopes) to wish the new couple a happy life and have a baby early.

After the wedding banquet, the couple will enter the marriage room. In the new house, the Chinese will light many red candles, and the couple will drink the cross-cupped wine. Finally, the husband will use a pole to lift the red bridal veil. This is the end of the busy formal wedding.

正式结婚之后，新人们还要完成一些婚后礼。结婚的第二天早晨，夫妻二人起床之后便要给父母敬茶，新郎新娘从此便改口，也将对方的父母称为父母。而妻子在一段时间之后，可以回到自己的娘家进行探望，这就是"归宁"。如此，漫长的结婚流程才真正结束。

等到夫妻生下宝宝的时候，中国人便会向亲朋好友赠送染红的鸡蛋，将喜庆分享给大家。孩子在满月、百天和周岁的时候，家中会举办各种各样的庆祝活动，比如满月酒、百日宴和周岁宴。在周岁宴上，中国人会让孩子进行抓周活动：把许许多多的小物品放在孩子面前，让孩子随便挑选，通过孩子抓取的东西，预测孩子未来的兴趣爱好和职业选择。

如今，中国人虽然学习了很多西方的婚礼样式，却仍然坚持着一些传统的婚礼习俗，只是省去了许多不必要的复杂流程。比如，人们仍然会身穿传统服饰拍结婚照、向父母和公婆敬茶、送出礼金和红包等，那些热闹的人群、喜庆的大红，也始终没有变过。

从父母之命到婚姻自由

在古代中国，男女结婚的年龄比较早，女方及笄（15岁），男方弱冠（20岁），就已经成年，便可以成亲了。除此之外，传统中国婚姻还有定娃娃亲、指

After a formal marriage, the couple will also complete the postmartial ceremony. On the morning of the second day of marriage, the couple will offer tea to their parents. They will call each other's parents "mother and father". After a period of time, the wife can return to her mother's home, which is called "guining". In this way, the long marriage process is completely over.

When the couple give birth to a baby, they are supposed to give red eggs to their relatives and friends to express their joy to everyone. When the baby is one month old, 100 days old, and one year old, there will be various celebrations, such as the full-month banquet, the hundred day banquet, and the first birthday banquet. At the first birthday banquet, the Chinese people will ask the baby to do the one-year-old catch (zhuazhou): putting a lot of small things in front of the baby, asking him or her to choose randomly and then predicting the baby's interests and career through the things the baby has catched.

Nowadays, Chinese people have learned a lot from Western wedding styles, but they still adhere to some traditional wedding customs and have omitted many unnecessary complicated processes. For example, people still wear traditional clothes to take wedding photos, offer tea to their parents and parents-in-law, give gifts and red envelopes, and so on. Moreover, those lively people and festive red have never changed.

From the Marriage Arranged by Parents to the Freedom of Marriage

In ancient China, men and women married at an early age. Women at 15 years old and men at 20 years old were already considered adults and could

腹为婚的做法。传统的婚姻一般是门当户对，要遵循父母之命，媒妁之言，就是男女双方的婚姻必须由父母做主，经媒人介绍。因此，有些新娘甚至结婚前没见过自己的新郎。

如今，根据中国法律规定，女方20岁、男方22周岁才可以结婚，这就保障了夫妻双方的受教育程度和组成家庭的经济能力。同时，法律保障自由婚姻，只要双方两情相悦，就可以办理结婚证，登记结婚。

中国的家庭结构

传统中国家庭讲究的是多子多福，儿孙满堂、四世同堂的景象是大家最乐意见到的。而夫妻二人也希望多生孩子，以此显得家族人丁兴旺。同时，中国传统社会重男轻女，每个家庭都希望生儿子，因为只有男子才有继承家产的权利，而女子则会在成年之后被嫁到其他家族。中国古代常以璋（玉器）瓦（纺

get married. In addition, the traditional Chinese also had the practice of child marriages and even arranging marriage between a boy and a girl when they were still in their mothers' bellies. Traditional marriages were usually matched and followed the arrangement of parents, along with the matchmaker's words; that is, the marriage of men and women must be decided by their parents and introduced by the matchmaker. Therefore, some brides might not have met their bridegrooms before they got married.

Nowadays, according to Chinese law, only when a woman is 20 years old and a man is 22 years old can she or he get married, which guarantees their educational level and economic ability to form a family. At the same time, the law guarantees freedom of marriage. As long as both parties are happy, they can apply for marriage certificates and register for marriage.

Chinese Family Structure

In the traditional Chinese concept, they believe that more children means more blessings. Children and grandchildren living in the same house or four generations living together in a big family is considered the happiest thing. The couple also hopes to have more children, so as to show the prosperity of the family. At the same time, in traditional Chinese society, men are more important than women. Every family wants to have a son, because only men have the right

锤）指代男女。生下男孩，则为弄璋之喜，暗示男孩如玉的品格；生下女孩，则为弄瓦之喜，暗示女孩将来胜任女工。因此，甚至有"弄璋得瓦"一词来表示家中没有生出男孩的失落之情。

而现代中国社会则截然不同。1982年开始，为了解决过于庞大的人口问题，中国实施计划生育政策，一个家庭只能拥有一个孩子，即"三口之家"。同时，男女平等，生男孩与生女孩享受一样的待遇。这就保证了女孩的受教育权利，使得中国的男女平权状况得到了越来越好的改善。2015年10月起，国家规定，一对夫妇可以生养两个孩子，因此，三口之家的家庭结构就此被打破。同时，中国的社会也变得越来越开放，在以往看来不可思议的单亲家庭、丁克家庭，现在也被越来越多的人所接受。中国的家庭结构变得越来越多样。

4. 重点词汇

订婚

在你们国家，**订婚**有特别的仪式吗？

to inherit the family's property, while women will be married to other families when they grow up. In ancient China, men and women were often referred to as jade and tiles, respectively. To give birth to a boy is called "to have the happiness of playing with jade", which implies the character of a boy is like jade, and to give birth to a girl is called "to have the happiness of playing with tile", suggesting that a girl will be competent for a knitting work in the future. Therefore, there is even a phrase "nong zhang de wa" (literally meaning wanting a piece of jade but getting a tile) to indicate that the family did not give birth to a boy, which brought the feelings of loss.

Modern Chinese society is quite different. Since 1982, in order to solve the huge population problem, China has implemented the family planning. A family can only have one child, what is thus called a "family of three". At the same time, men and women are equal, and giving birth to a boy or a girl receives the same treatment. This guarantees girls' right to education and makes the situation of equal rights between men and women in China more progressive. Since October 2015, the Chinese government has stipulated that a couple can have two children, so the family structure of a family of three has been broken. At the same time, China's society is becoming more and more open. The incredible single-parent family and the DINK family in the past are now accepted by more and more people. Chinese family structure has become more and more diverse.

4. Keywords

engagement

Are there any special rituals for **engagement** in your country?

成亲

成亲在现代汉语中是什么意思？

重男轻女

为什么人们会有"**重男轻女**"的观念？

计划生育

计划生育是什么意思？中国为什么要实行**计划生育**？

5. 实践活动

（1）看一看下图的结婚证，告诉同学上面包含哪些信息。

getting married

What does **"getting married"** mean in modern Chinese?

prefer boys to girls

Why do people have the concept of "**preferring boys to girls**"?

family planning

What does **family planning** mean? Why did China adopt **family planning**?

5. Activities

(1) Look at the marriage certificate below and tell your classmates what information it contains.

持 证 人

　　XXX

登记日期

　　XXXX年XX月XX日

结婚证字号

　　XXXXXXXXX

备注

姓名 XXX　　　　　　性别 男
国籍 中国　　　　　　出生日期 XXXX年X月X日
身份证件号 XXXXXXXXX

姓名 XXX　　　　　　性别 女
国籍 中国　　　　　　出生日期 XXXX年X月X日
身份证件号 XXXXXXXXX

（2）现代中国有许多年轻人采用中西混合的方式举办婚礼，即以西式婚礼结婚，再以中式服饰敬酒。查阅一些资料，并且与同学讨论一下，分析这种现象产生的原因，说一说你对这种现象的看法。

（3）古代中国社会的婚姻都是"父母之命，媒妁之言"，几乎没有自由恋爱。为什么会有这种现象？请分析。

（4）对比下面两张图，说一说中西方婚礼有哪些不同。

（5）研究一下中国的户口本，看看上面登记了哪些信息。

(2) In modern China, many young people hold weddings in a mixture of Chinese and Western ways, i.e. weddings in Western style and toasts in Chinese costumes. Look for some information and discuss it with your classmates. Analyze the causes of this phenomenon and give your views on it.

(3) Ancient Chinese society advocated marriages of "the arrangement of parents and the matchmaker's words", with almost no free love. Why did this happen? Please analyze.

(4) Compare the two pictures below and tell the differences between Chinese and Western weddings.

(5) Study the Chinese household register and see what information it contains.

常 住 人 口 登 记 卡				
姓　　　　名	ＸＸＸ	户 主 或 与户 主 关 系	父子	
曾　用　名		性　　　别	男	
出　生　地	××省××市××区	民　　　族	汉族	
籍　　　贯	××省××市××区	出 生 日 期	××××年××月××日	
本市(县)其它住址		宗教信仰		
公民身份证件编号	××××××××××××	身　高	172	血 型　不明
文 化 程 度	本科	婚姻状况　未婚	兵役状况	未服兵役
服 务 处 所	ＸＸＸＸ	职　　业	工人	
何 时 由 何 地迁 来 本 市(县)				
何时由何地迁来本址				
承办人签章：×××		登记日期：××××年××月××日		

（6）中国拥有比较严格的户籍制度，户口与当地生活有比较密切的关系。请查阅相关资料，了解现代中国户口管理的变化。

6. 自我评估

	😊	😐	☹️
（1）我知道中西婚礼的异同。			
（2）我能说出中国古今婚礼的相关习俗及其变化。			
（3）我能说出中国家庭结构的变化。			

(6) China has a stricter household registration system, which is closely related to local life. Please find the relevant information to understand the changes of household registration management in modern China.

6. Self-assessment

	😃	😐	☹️
(1) I know the similarities and differences between Chinese and Western weddings.			
(2) I can tell the relevant customs and changes of Chinese ancient and modern weddings.			
(3) I can tell the change of Chinese family structure.			